Arguing for Equality

Arguing for Equality

JOHN BAKER

VERSO

London · New York

First published by Verso 1987
© John Baker

Verso
UK: 6 Meard Street, London W1V 3HR
USA: 29 West 35th Street, New York, NY 10001 2291

Verso is the imprint of New Left Books

British Library Cataloguing in Publication Data
Baker, John, 1950–
  Arguing for equality
  1. Equality
  I. Title
  305   HM146

US Library of Congress Cataloging-in-Publication Data
Baker, John, 1950–
  Arguing for equality.
  Bibliography: p.
  Includes index.
  1. Equality. I. Title.
JC575.B34   1987   323.4'01   87-14990

ISBN 0-86091-182-9
ISBN 0-86091-895-5 (pbk.)

Typeset by Columns of Reading
Printed in Great Britain by Biddles Ltd, Guildford

For Isabel

Contents

Acknowledgements

I have learnt more about equality than I can say from students at University College, Dublin: my thanks to them. I'd also like to thank Steve Bodington, Attracta Dunlop, Norman Geras, Sam Guttenplan, Brian Harrison, Bruce Landesman, Richard Lindley, Ed O'Callaghan, Jennifer Todd, David Wasserstein, Petrena Williams, and Tim Wilson for reading the whole book and making extensive comments, as well as for a lot of encouragement. I'm very grateful as well to Bernard Bourdillon, Jerry Cohen, Jean Collins, Sacha Craddock, Sally Craddock, Keith Dowling, Jamie Gough, Corinne Perleman, and Dave Taylor for reading and commenting on various chapters. Thanks, too, to participants at meetings sponsored by the Irish Philosophical Society, the Political Studies Association of Ireland, the Royal Irish Academy, and the London School of Economics Department of Government, at which parts of this book were tried out. I am grateful to Birkbeck College Department of Philosophy for facilitating my work during 1984-85, to University College, Dublin for granting me sabbatical leave, and to the British Academy and Royal Irish Academy for financial assistance. Thanks of a different, first book kind are due to many, but especially to Alice and Roger Baker, Edwin Barlow, and Peter Hacker.

Arguing for equality is a collective task, and I hope that the people listed above, as well as many of the authors cited in 'References and Further Reading', will recognize their contribution to this book. I have no desire to claim the ideas here as my own personal property: their strength lies in the political tradition they express. But nor should anyone assume that they are held by all the people I have mentioned.

How to Use this Book

The aim of this book is to set out the central arguments for equality, and to reply to the arguments commonly raised against it. A central theme is that true equality depends on a democratic population who think and decide for themselves. Thus, this book is designed to be clear and easy to use, to avoid unnecessary jargon, and to stimulate people to draw on their own experience, make up their own minds and develop their own ideas. In today's political climate, many people have lost their sympathy for equality – I hope that the arguments in this book will help to reawaken it. I also hope to help committed egalitarians to define their own views.

The book is in two parts. I begin Part One by trying to explain what it actually means to believe in equality – to be an egalitarian. I then set out the basic case for equality, drawing on the ideas of basic needs, mutual respect, and a sense of community. These are natural starting points for any egalitarian argument. In Part Two, I consider more controversial areas, in which both egalitarians and their opponents claim to have support. Each chapter is relatively self-contained, disposing of some commonplace objections to equality and extending the case in its favour. I argue that we must go beyond the limited equality involved in 'equal opportunity'; that the privileged cannot claim to deserve their advantages; that freedom and equality support one another; that equality would benefit society as a whole; and that equality is possible. A few miscellaneous objections are discussed in Chapter 10, and the last chapter summarizes the argument and draws some practical political conclusions.

Each chapter tries to discuss general arguments first. The last section of each chapter contains replies to specific objections which may or may not bother you.

I have tried to write in plain English that can be understood by anyone interested in equality. Inevitably, there are some technical terms, as well as some key concepts which are used more precisely than in everyday speech. Political argument is generally conducted in obscure terms which few people understand and which are used to impress and intimidate opponents. The glossary here is merely intended to dispel some of the fog, not to insult anyone's intelligence.

There's a section called 'Do-It-Yourself Equality' towards the end of the book. Although light-hearted in tone, its intention is perfectly serious – to encourage the critical, independent thinking which people with money, status, and power have every reason to suppress. Political argument can be difficult even if you try to make it clear. That's no reason for it to be boring as well.

This book has deliberate limitations. First of all, it's not a book on either economics or political science – it doesn't pursue the question of how, in detail, a more egalitarian economic or political system would be organized. It's concerned with arguments for the fundamental principles these systems should be based on. So broadly speaking it expresses a political philosophy rather than a political programme, and discusses economics and political institutions only where these raise important matters of principle. My philosophical method is fairly straightforward, since I don't go in for supposedly ultimate foundations for equality which are usually difficult to understand and even harder to agree with. Instead, I start with a number of the values you'd find in the beliefs of ordinary women and men, and argue that anyone who believes in these values ought to believe in equality as well. The main reasons for this approach are given in Chapter 10.

A related limitation is that I avoid trying to answer every question for egalitarianism, concentrating instead on defending central ideas. Egalitarians can genuinely disagree on many issues without weakening their overall case for a more equal society. Since it's in the interests of equality itself that these issues should be raised and discussed, I sometimes do raise them without attempting to deal with them conclusively.

Finally, this book doesn't try to plug every possible gap in every argument. I've tried to deal with common and important arguments and objections, not every imaginable one. 'References and Further Reading' is a guide to my sources, and to some works which go beyond the limits of this book.

I hope you'll find what follows interesting and enjoyable, that you'll find arguments you disagree with or could have expressed better, and that you'll emerge with your own ideas, more or less different from mine. This book couldn't be put to a better use.

PART ONE

The Basic Case
For Equality

1

What Egalitarians Believe

Imagine a country with no poverty. No one sleeps under bridges; no one looks through garbage for food. On the contrary: everyone has what you or I would call a decent home and a decent standard of living. There's no division into rich and poor, and anyone in a position of authority is democratically elected. Since people's work is meaningful and satisfying, they aren't compelled to do jobs they hate. Neither is anyone snubbed or patronized for belonging to the wrong class, or forced to bow and scrape. Women and men treat each other as equals; skin colour is irrelevant to your prospects in life; and you don't have to suffer for being Irish or Jewish or disabled or gay.

That would be a society of equals: the kind of society this book recommends. Today, it exists only in the imagination, and the belief in equality is out of fashion. But I shall argue that an equal society is both possible and desirable. The first step in that argument is to state more precisely what equality is. Then I'll say a little more about what an egalitarian society might look like.

Equality Defined

No simple definition of equality will do. Certainly, equality doesn't mean that everybody is or should be the same: people are different, and long may they remain so. Nor does it simply

3

mean equality for women or black people. These are egalitarian aims, but not the only ones. Equality is sometimes taken to mean equality of income, but that won't do, either. Anyone can see that it costs more to satisfy some people's needs than others' – for instance, the needs of paraplegics versus people who can walk. Surely those people with greater need should have more income than others; equality of income would be wrong.

Equality is a complicated idea. For that reason, it helps to think of it not as a single principle at all, but as the following group of principles. These seem to me to be the central beliefs of today's egalitarians, and the principles this book sets out to defend. I will call them the principles of equality.

Basic needs

Every person has the right to the satisfaction of her or his basic needs. Egalitarians believe that it is completely indefensible for some to live in luxury while others face utter deprivation. Beyond this, they look forward to a society in which everyone has not just a bearable, but a satisfying, fulfilling life.

Equal respect

Most immediately, egalitarians oppose any form of degrading treatment or circumstances. But they also reject both the snobbery and patronizing attitudes of the privileged, and the feelings of deference and inferiority which they foster – the status hierarchy by which people are appreciated not for their personal qualities but for their social position. Egalitarians look towards the development of a society in which everyone has an equal social status, and in which people relate to each other on the basis of fellow-feeling or community instead of grouping themselves into social and economic pyramids.

Economic equality

Egalitarians oppose the huge differences in income and wealth found both within countries and between them. It's not that everyone should have exactly the same income, since people have different needs and aspirations. But much more equality of income is certainly in order. Egalitarians also seek equality in production, involving democratic control of the economy and of the workplace, and the right of everyone not just to some kind of work, but to work which is safe, dignified, useful, and engaging. If there is boring, exhausting, and disagreeable work to be done, it should be shared out more equally, and the people who do it should be compensated. As for 'equality of opportunity', that shouldn't be an equal start in the rat race, but the provision to everyone of ways to develop their individual talents in a satisfying and fulfilling way.

Political equality

There is more to political equality than the formal right to vote and to stand for office – though these are certainly important. Egalitarians defend civil rights like free speech and free assembly, but also call for institutions which give formal freedoms real bite, and which give their members equal power. That requires a thorough and imaginative extension of democratic participation in government, industry, education, social services, family life: a participation which promotes real freedom from arbitrary power and oppression, and through which people can exercise a much greater control over the shapes of their own lives.

Sexual, racial, ethnic, and religious equality

Egalitarians are opposed to treating some people worse than others because of their sex or sexual preference, their colour or culture, their religion or lack of it. They condemn blatant discrimination, as in racial segregation and religious per-secution, but they also reject the sexism, racism, and intolerance which lead to systematic differences of wealth, power, and status. More generally, egalitarians oppose any form of discrimination based on irrelevant differences – for instance, discrimination against someone who is old or disabled.

Grouping the principles of equality under five overlapping headings is just a matter of convenience. You might prefer a larger or smaller number. A useful three-way division corresponding to the major inequalities in our own society is 'equality of wealth, status, and power'. The important point to remember is that equality is a complex idea.

What Would an Equal Society Look Like?

Every society has within it certain structures or patterns of relations: for instance, the way its economy operates, its political process, its religious and cultural life, its family networks, its system of education, and so on. These are its social institutions, and arguments about equality are arguments about some of the principles which ought to shape these institutions. Arguments for equality are in this sense *prior* to decisions about particular social institutions, such as the choice between capitalism and socialism or between selective and comprehensive schools. They provide principles on which those institutional decisions are based. But since egalitarianism is associated with certain institutions it is worth saying a little about them at the start. Later chapters will illustrate and expand on some of the general points made here.

Capitalism, socialism, and equality

In modern politics, egalitarians have been associated with socialism and anti-egalitarians with capitalism or 'free enterprise'. Socialism is sometimes even *defined* in terms of equality. On the other hand, defenders of capitalism have been known to argue that socialism is authoritarian (and hence contrary to political equality), and that a freely operating capitalism does or would promote a degree of economic equality. So is 'socialism versus capitalism' the same issue as 'equality versus inequality' or not?

One certainty is that egalitarianism cannot be identified with wholesale support for existing 'socialist' countries such as the USSR, China, Cuba, and the countries of eastern Europe. Some egalitarians would defend some of the programmes of these countries, such as their dramatic advances in literacy, health, and social welfare, and would even defend some of the costs involved. But none of these societies is a model of equality. There are too many power inequalities for that, not to mention income inequalities. But then, these countries are not regarded by many western socialists as a model of *socialism* either, for much the same reason. Typically, these countries are considered inegalitarian in spite of their socialist elements, because they haven't gone far enough in the direction of democratic control. Their commitment to socialism is seen as half-hearted or distorted or constrained by circumstances. Capitalist countries, on the other hand, are believed by most egalitarians to be unequal *because* of their capitalism. For although it can be argued that capitalism has helped to bring about certain kinds of equality, it seems to require other inequalities by its very nature, whether in regard to the basic contract between employer and worker, or power relations at work, or the role of the state, or the distribution of income and wealth.

Theoretically, it's possible to separate the issue of equality from the issue of socialism by defining socialism as a democratically planned economy in which the means of production are under social ownership, and leaving open the question of whether such an economy is necessary for equality. But politically, equality and socialism share the same platform. The connection becomes especially obvious when you see people using arguments against socialism as reasons for opposing equality. It would be unrealistic to ignore these arguments on the pretence that socialism and equality are different issues. Thus the aim of this book is to argue for equality, but many of its arguments are for socialism, too.

In a socialist society, many decisions now taken by the owners and controllers of capital would be taken by the state. But it would be quite wrong to think that a socialist state would try to control absolutely everything. For socialism would involve a strong commitment to industrial democracy and could include a variety of forms of common ownership. Industries and services owned by the state could be organized nationally, regionally, or locally, and would have a democratic management. There could be many kinds of workers' and consumers' cooperatives, too. A socialist economy might also have room for certain limited forms of private business. None of these involve the kind of rigid state control often associated with socialism.

More generally, egalitarians are quite capable of distinguishing between those equalities which it is reasonable to use power to achieve and those which should only be the result of discussion and consensus. For instance, it's reasonable to legislate against severely cruel or degrading treatment without thinking that every way in which one person humiliates another is a fit object of legal interference. It may be part of the egalitarian ideal for people always to treat each other as equals, but it is also part of that ideal for people to have power

8

over their own lives. In this as in many other cases you have to decide on your priorities.

Anti-egalitarians are fond of implying that in an egalitarian society every aspect of life would be regulated by the state, every breach of equality punishable by secret police – as if there were no inequalities in that! This is a travesty of egalitarianism, as the arguments in this book will show.

Equality and democracy

Democracy is central to any egalitarian society. Egalitarians cherish the democratic freedoms established in many western countries and want to extend them. For nobody can deny that democracy is still very limited. There are vast areas of life, particularly in the economy, in which ordinary people have no say at all, while in other areas the degree of popular participation and power is minimal. In societies marked by huge inequalities of wealth, power, and status, it is inevitable that some people will have more influence than others, that the wealthy will have greater control over government policy than the poor, that the well-to-do will be better informed and more active in politics than the average citizen. The egalitarian answer to these problems is to attack the basic inequalities of condition which cause them.

This fundamental commitment to democracy stands in complete contrast to the widespread idea that an egalitarian society would be run by a bureaucratic elite, who would decide what people needed, what would be produced, the distribution of incomes, and so on. Anti-egalitarians point to the size and power of even today's tax, social security, housing, and social work bureaucracies. which are at least supposed to create a more equal society. But they seem to ignore the huge bureaucracies which run the military forces, the road network, the courts, prisons, customs and immigration, which can hardly be blamed on equality. Nor is bureaucracy limited to public institutions. Any employee of a large organization, any consumer complaining to a big company, anyone borrowing money from a bank or building society, knows about bureaucracies, some well-organized and responsive, others not. Even if egalitarians did expect lots of decisions over production and income to be taken by bureaucrats, how different would that be from the way we live now, where the

boards of management taking these decisions are just as hard
to influence?

But egalitarianism is not a charter for bureaucrats. In fact,
the very argument against bureaucratic power is the egalitarian
commitment to democracy. That means both democratic
control over whatever administrative bodies are unavoidable
and the attempt to restructure institutions so that decisions are
made by the people they affect. For instance, there needs to
be much more involvement by both health workers and
patients in the way hospitals and medical services are designed
and run; more participation by both municipal workers and
local residents in the management of local services. It ought to
be remembered as well that many of the worst excesses of
supposedly egalitarian bureaucracies, such as social welfare
snoopers and complicated and obscure rules for grants and
allowances, derive not from their egalitarianism but from the
limits placed on them by an unequal society. The bureaucrats
are there to make sure that the poor don't get too much –
where 'too much' is far less than equality would demand.

Egalitarians do talk about the *distribution* of income, wealth
and power, but that doesn't mean that these things ought to be
distributed by a bureaucracy. Bureaucracies are one of many
kinds of social institution, all of which affect the way income,
wealth, power and so on are spread across society. Markets,
inheritance and gifts also influence the distribution of income,
wealth, and power. And since all these social institutions are
socially created and open to alteration, it is perfectly
legitimate to ask whether there is any justification for them.
For that you need the sort of general principles which this
book is concerned to defend.

Equality and the welfare state

For nearly a century, equality has been linked with the idea of
the 'welfare state': income support for the elderly, unemployed
and disabled; publicly provided education for all, with a trend
in the direction of comprehensive, mixed-ability schooling; a
free, comprehensive health service, at least for the worst off;
public housing for people on low incomes; and a variety of
social services for people with special needs. Would an
egalitarian society mean more of the same? Since the welfare

state does stand for more equality than 'free market' alternatives offered by its opponents, there are certainly good reasons for supporting and defending it. But there are two major reasons why an egalitarian society might turn out to be very different.

First of all is the issue of democratic control. The present welfare state is a compromise which suits many interests. It helps people in need, but it also helps to keep them in their place. It is a system of support but also of control. In some areas, particularly in housing, users and providers of public services are starting to cooperate in making the system more democratic, but there's a long way to go. Too much of the system still runs on the belief that the bureaucrats know best and that consumers should be grateful for whatever they're given.

The second reason is that the welfare state is designed for an unequal society. Many of its policies and problems would be transformed by more equality. For instance, there's a lot of argument in education over how to promote equality of opportunity in an unequal society. There are bitter conflicts over the use of limited funds, with parents fighting over the means to protect their children's futures. Schooling is seen as a major cause of achievement in adult life, and since all children are in competition for advancement there is no limit to the demand for educational resources. Even a good school could be better, making a crucial difference to children's educational success. No wonder there are disputes over private schooling, mixed-ability classes, examination systems, busing! In an egalitarian society, there would still be disagreements over the best ways to ensure that every person had the opportunity to develop their ability in a satisfying and fulfilling way and over how to use our resources – disagreements that it would be impossible to sort out now. But there wouldn't be conflict over access to privilege; the penalty for 'failure' wouldn't be poverty; there wouldn't be a contrast between inner city ghettos and middle class suburbs.

Undoubtedly the welfare state provides some of the materials for the social institutions of an egalitarian society, as well as a great deal of experience in providing for people's needs. But it would be wrong to imagine that an equal society would just be a bigger welfare state. It would be in many ways a different society altogether.

How Far Should Equality Go?

Politically, egalitarianism usually focuses on particular societies or countries, but it can have a much broader or narrower scope. Broader, in pursuing equalities among all the people on earth (and, for some egalitarians, among all higher forms of life). Narrower, in seeking equalities within clubs or workplaces or religions or personal relationships. Just as egalitarianism has many aspects, it has many contexts. Is it wrong to seek equality in one country but not between countries? To look for equality with one's friends but not with strangers?

This is partly a question of principle, and partly one of tactics. In principle, most of the arguments for equality are quite general, and apply at least to all people; but the arguments based on a sense of community discussed in Chapter 4 provide some ground for localism, as do issues of planning discussed in Chapter 8. Tactically, the argument for localism is that you can be more effective within your own country than in another one; the argument for globalism is that what's possible in one country is very strongly limited by what's happening around it. These tactical questions are addressed briefly at the end of Chapter 9. In this book, the emphasis will be on arguments for equality within a single country. That doesn't mean that other equalities are unimportant.

Equality and Social Justice

The purpose of the next three chapters is to state three central grounds for the principles of equality: the satisfaction of needs, respect for others, and a sense of community. Together, they establish the basic case for equality which serves as a backdrop for the arguments of Part Two. In the rest of this chapter, I consider some objections to the way I've defined equality. The layout is intended to help you to locate the objections you're interested in and to skip the ones you're not.

Why can't egalitarianism be defined simply as a belief in social justice? Isn't that the issue which distinguishes it from its opponents?

It's true that egalitarians are much more fond of the term 'social justice' than anti-egalitarians – so much so, that social justice is practically a synonym for equality. But there's another way of looking at the matter, which takes equality to be only one of a number of 'conceptions' or 'theories' of social justice – including the theory that everyone should get what they deserve, or the theory that justice consists in respecting people's property rights. According to this 'many theories' view, someone who merely claims to believe in social justice isn't really saying very much. I don't want to deny the importance for equality of having won rhetorical control over the term 'social justice', and I wouldn't discourage anyone from thinking of this book as an argument not just for one conception of social justice, but for social justice itself. But it seems less confusing overall to express things in terms of equality instead.

There's a secondary issue here, too. The idea of justice is closely connected with the idea of rights, and both with ideas of forcing or at least demanding certain kinds of behaviour. It seems to me that only some of the principles of equality, though perhaps the most important ones, are matters of rights. Others describe a social ideal which depends on free consent. I haven't drawn a sharp line between them, but talking in terms of *justice* seems to put them all on one side.

Isn't it cheating to talk about many 'principles of equality'? Egalitarians are supposed to believe in Equality, so shouldn't they have some particular equality in mind? Otherwise they just don't know what they're talking about.

This objection takes an over-simplistic view of the way people can use words like 'equality' to mean different things in different situations. In ordinary political discussion, the context normally makes it clear what people are talking about when they speak for or against equality: whether it's to do with sexual equality or political equality or equality of income or status. It's when you start to *theorize* about equality that you start thinking that all these uses have to be based on some single underlying principle. But why should they be based on anything more than the fact that they're all about particular equalities?

But if there's more than one principle of equality, then the principles can conflict; and unless egalitarians say how to resolve these conflicts, they haven't really specified what they believe in.

The general position of egalitarians is that the principles do not conflict, at least not in any major way. Later chapters reveal just how true this is: for instance, Chapters 7 and 8 show that both political equality and the satisfaction of needs actually depend on economic equality. Of course, the principles of equality are very broad, and are bound to involve some minor conflicts. As they stand, they don't give a precise answer to every question of social policy. But that doesn't make them useless – they're clear enough, and consistent enough with each other, to state a recognizable political outlook.

The principles listed aren't really principles of equality. In particular, some of them are really principles of universal entitlement. For instance, the principles that everyone should have their basic needs satisfied, and that everyone should have satisfying and fulfilling work.

The reply to this objection is that principles of universal entitlement have always been part of the egalitarian tradition, because what they criticize are states of affairs in which some people enjoy a certain good and others are denied it; that is, situations of partial entitlement. This is not to say that any principle of universal entitlement is egalitarian, any more than that any principle of equal distribution is. It is merely to say that principles of this form have as much of a claim to being called egalitarian as any other.

2

Human Needs

First and foremost, everyone's basic needs should be satisfied. This simple principle unites egalitarians world-wide, and it justifies many other equalities. That's what makes it one of the three basic grounds for equality dealt with in the next three chapters. For how can any society turn its back on the needs of its members? How can any of us disregard the needs of fellow human beings? Yet to pay attention to those needs implies a commitment to the wellbeing of others which extends to every area of equality.

But what are people's basic needs? Do people need everything they say they do? Do we need more today than our grandparents did? Listening to everyday talk, you'll hear people say they need all kinds of things. Water is needed for washing and drinking, and ultimately for staying alive. Neckties are needed for getting into certain restaurants, lemons for eating smoked salmon. Anything you care to mention is needed for one thing or another. Doesn't the satisfaction of needs become an impossible and ridiculous aim?

When egalitarians talk about *basic* needs they have a rather more distinct idea in mind. What they usually concentrate on are the things people need to live, and beyond that to live 'decently', to lead a 'normal' life. That means the things without which people would be suffering, ill, or failing to cope: things like food, clothing, and shelter; clean water and public sanitation; personal security and dignity; supportive relations with others and privacy. Those needs are recognized by everyone. Egalitarians sometimes also talk about 'higher needs', and have in mind the things people need to grow, to develop, to thrive, like a stimulating education, satisfying work, understanding friends. These, too, are needs which no one would deny. But issues about needs aren't always so straightforward, and raise two general problems worth considering.

Disagreements About Needs

One problem is that people sometimes disagree over what's needed for a decent or a thriving life. Sometimes they agree on an ultimate aim, but disagree on the means: a good example is the conflict between people who believe in 'alternative medicine' and people who don't. A different kind of disagreement is over the very idea of a decent life – over conceptions of human wellbeing. What are the contributions of individuality and of community to human growth? To what extent does personal development depend on following our deepest natural inclinations, and to what extent on mastering them? Do people find more fulfilment in worldly achievement or in mystical devotion? An egalitarian society would have to cope with such disagreements, but how?

The first thing to remember is that in practice there is a great deal of consensus over basic needs. Relief workers in Africa don't have to probe deep philosophical questions to discover that certain things are needed: those needs are immediate and obvious. Water boards aim to provide everyone with clean water and effective sanitation, needs which no one doubts. Even when there's disagreement, it's sometimes possible for people to respect each other's claims of need, and to share responsibility for satisfying them. Thus, one person's idea of a full life may involve a commitment to the fine arts, another's to popular music, another's to sport, yet each can accept the validity of the others' ideals and hence of their claims on social resources.

People aren't always so compatible. Sometimes they disagree strongly over their conceptions of a good life. In those circumstances, it would be unreasonable to expect them to accept responsibility for the claims of need they reject. And so not even an egalitarian society can commit itself to providing all the things people say they need. But it might find ways of allowing people to obtain these things through their own efforts. In practical terms, that means letting people choose to work harder than others in return for higher incomes. Within the limits set by other egalitarian principles, such income inequalities would be a legitimate expression of differences in need.

Thus, disagreement over needs isn't as serious a problem for egalitarianism as it seems. But it would be wrong to imply that a society of equals could facilitate every possible conception of human wellbeing. For instance, egalitarians cannot assent to anyone's 'need' to dominate others, or to live in idle luxury; they cannot accept the belief that the mass of humanity need 'authority' and hierarchy. Those 'needs' could only be satisfied in an unequal society. Fortunately, there is plenty of evidence that people can have happy, fulfilling lives without being insatiable consumers, power-mad oppressors, or obedient sheep.

Needs which Vary from One Society to Another

A second problem with 'need' is social variation. Do we need more than the Victorians? Do New Yorkers need more than New Guineans? Or do all human beings have the same basic needs? Drawing on the arguments so far, we can see that some of the things people in rich societies say they need are not really needed, or at least not very urgently. Video machines may make life more fun, but they aren't necessary simply for coping and staying healthy. But other differences between societies are more genuine. For different societies make different *demands*, put different obstacles in the way of surviving and coping. Thus, it's sometimes said that 'poor people in America would be rich anywhere else'. But they *aren't* anywhere else: they are in a country where their poverty makes them despised and rejected, destroys their families, undermines their sense of their own worth, divides them from the rest of the community, drives them into alcoholism and drug addiction. Those are conditions of need every bit as real as the hunger and homelessness which many Americans suffer as well.

Different societies may also have different dominant conceptions of a good life – one perhaps more spiritual, another more materialistic – and these differences will themselves lead to different basic needs. For example, in today's America many people need cars. Their society has created a particular image of a decent life, and has so structured its arrangements for living and working that without a car that life is unattainable. As with differences among individuals, a society with a particularly expensive conception of the good life will claim to have expensive needs; but it cannot justifiably expect other societies, with other conceptions of life, to pay for them.

Thus, people in different societies do have different needs. But societies can be changed: we could satisfy the needs of Americans *either* by producing cars *or* by restructuring life and work. Equality does not entail accepting things as they stand.

If a society is so structured that some of its people's needs can't possibly be met, or that fulfilling the needs of its own population can only be achieved by frustrating the needs of others, then need provides a strong reason for radical change. For instance, Marx argued that capitalism *requires* poverty, to keep wages low so that profits can be made. And poverty prevents people in capitalist societies from leading what capitalism inevitably portrays as a decent life. That provides a need-based argument against capitalism.

Why Care about Needs?

The two problems of disagreement and social variation are standard points in anti-egalitarian argument, because the case for caring about basic needs is itself so obvious. Having disposed of the objections, it's worth reviewing the case in favour.

A person's wellbeing depends on her or his needs being satisfied. But for most of us a concern for other people's wellbeing is a matter of common decency, a basic moral requirement. So for most of us it's a matter of common decency to be concerned about whether people's needs are satisfied. For the same reason, it's clear that people's most urgent needs – the ones they would suffer most from not satisfying – should be given priority over less urgent needs. Since the argument depends on the idea of wellbeing, it loses its force when people have radically different views about what wellbeing is.

The central importance of people's most urgent or basic needs is part of the reason egalitarians talk about a *right* to their satisfaction, and say that this isn't just a matter of charity but of *justice*. People suffering from hunger, disease, and poverty shouldn't have to beg for help, they can demand it. This right to satisfy basic needs isn't necessarily the right to a hand-out, since in an egalitarian society each person would contribute as well as benefit. Each would share the collective responsibility for satisfying everyone's needs.

Concern for wellbeing is the fundamental argument for satisfying needs, but there are many others. A willingness to allow people's basic needs to go unsatisfied betrays a gross contempt for them as people: an attitude that they are beneath consideration. A lack of commitment to satisfying needs prevents the development of a sense of community and common interest, and it reinforces resistance to change, since the cost of change for the rich and powerful becomes not just a lower standard of living but the risk of poverty. Need is rarely self-inflicted: when one person's need results from other people's greed, it deserves to be remedied. Even self-interest provides a reason for satisfying needs, since social groups or classes deprived of their basic needs are at best handicapped in their ability to contribute to social and economic progress and at worst dangerous. The arguments for satisfying needs are compelling.

Beyond Need to Other Equalities

Suppose you agree that basic needs should be satisfied. Does that give you any reason to believe in the other principles of equality? There are two arguments that it does. First, it's unlikely that people's basic needs can be satisfied unless the other principles are followed. What society will provide for the needs of its social outcasts? Only people who are respected as equals can expect to have their needs taken seriously. Economic inequality also has bad effects on needs, since it shifts production from needs to luxuries and shapes the economy to protect the privileged. Political inequality prevents people from expressing their needs; it produces bureaucratic and patronizing welfare services which often frustrate people's real needs. Sexual, racial, ethnic, and religious inequalities are obvious recipes for denying the needs of the groups they affect. Thus, only a fully egalitarian society could be relied upon to satisfy everyone's basic needs.

The second argument seems just as straightforward. The main reason for caring about needs in the first place is a wider concern for other people's wellbeing. Morally speaking, that concern has to be impartial. It seems to follow that we ought to pursue *equal* wellbeing, and that that's what equality is all about.

But the argument won't quite do. If you are badly hurt by the death of a close friend, should everyone else suffer in the name of equal wellbeing? We ought to comfort you and try to make life easier for you for a while, but that doesn't bring us all to the same level. The principle of equal wellbeing would involve the worst kind of 'levelling down'.

In any case, overall wellbeing is in many ways beyond the reach of social planning. For wellbeing is affected by many things: by whether you find satisfaction in the things you are capable of doing, rather than frustration at your limitations; whether you find lasting and fulfilling personal relationships; whether you or those close to you suffer tragic accidents or illnesses; and so on. You can't control *everything*: at least, not without making life worse, not better. Another objection to equal wellbeing has already been mentioned: the fact that people have different conceptions of wellbeing. Suppose your idea of a happy life is to travel to every country in the world. Equality of wellbeing would seem to require the rest of us to bankroll your ambitions, since otherwise you'd be much more miserable than we were. If we were wonderfully generous we might choose to help you out, but you could hardly complain if we didn't. All you can reasonably expect are the same options for pursuing your aims as are offered to everyone else.

It makes sense, then, for egalitarians to adopt a more sophisticated attitude towards wellbeing. What's really necessary is to provide everyone with the material and institutional means with which they could reasonably expect to have a satisfying life, and to give people the opportunity to develop their own conceptions of wellbeing and to live their own lives. That would have to include the satisfaction of basic needs, the granting of mutual respect, and the right to a say in important decisions. It would mean establishing a minimum income, sharing the hardships of socially necessary toil, offering to everyone the prospect of safe and engaging work, and providing, if possible, the option to work more or less than average for more or less income. It would rule out social structures which systematically favour men over women, white people over black, Christians over Jews, and so on. A little reflection suggests that even allowing for different personal ideals and for different choices about work, the conditions necessary for one person to live a good life would be pretty similar to those for another, so that differences in net income and wealth need not be very great. This is the real but complicated connection between need, wellbeing, and the principles of equality.

Ecology, Egoism, and Experts

With a complicated idea like need, objections can spring from many different directions. This section looks at a few common complaints.

Why make such a big deal out of the satisfaction of basic needs? Surely every society satisfies the basic needs of its members – otherwise it wouldn't exist in the first place!

It's true that each society has to satisfy the most basic needs of most of its members just to keep going, but there are lots of examples of societies in which some people are allowed simply to starve, or to die of exposure or of a curable disease. In any case, the commitment to satisfying basic needs goes beyond mere subsistence needs, to the conditions for living a decent life – for coping with life, not just surviving. No one can argue that every society satisfies those needs; certainly not our own.

What if we can't satisfy people's needs? The world only has limited resources, and there may not be enough to go around. Trying to satisfy everyone's needs just leads to programmes of economic growth which destroy the environment and cause deeper crises later.

It's true that many societies on their own cannot satisfy their members' needs, because of their internal structures and their place in the world's economic system. But the world as a whole does have the resources, if only they were used properly. For instance, the United Nations Food and Agriculture Organization estimates that the world's agricultural output exceeds its dietary requirements by more than ten per cent; even within poor countries there's an excess of production over requirements. What's wrong is how food gets distributed: the poorest people simply can't afford it.

That's not to pretend that resources aren't limited, or to endorse economic growth as the answer to need. Easy access to birth control, the use of alternative technologies, decentralization, health education, and other 'green' policies are plausible alternatives. Choosing among these approaches requires a lot of technical knowledge, but must also be guided by principles. That's the role of the principles of equality.

It's simply not true to say that we're all obliged as a matter of morality to promote the wellbeing of others. We may have some obligations to our family and friends, but we don't owe anything to strangers.

A lot of the history of moral philosophy has been taken up with trying to prove that we do have an obligation to care about others, and the arguments are still going on. In this book, I am assuming that concern for others is a matter of common decency, and I believe that most people would agree. In any case, the central issue here is with principles concerning the shape of a society as a whole, not (in the first instance, anyway) with how each of us ought individually to treat others: and when you think about such principles, you have to be impartial. The question of our *personal* obligations is taken up in Chapter 10.

Talking about needs is all very well, but who's supposed to decide who needs what? Are we all supposed to put ourselves into the hands of experts?

There are of course some distinct areas such as medicine and nutrition in which experts can advise us on what we need, though even these areas are controversial. But who can claim to be an expert on the question of what makes for a decent or a fulfilling life? Or on the tremendous variety of styles of living? The egalitarian principle of political equality makes it quite clear that people ought to make up their own minds on what they need. They can be argued with, and you don't always have to accept their assertions of need. But disagreement is a feature of many areas of social life. It's not always resolved by experts.

All these arguments seem to assume the overriding value of material things. But most needs aren't material at all. Egalitarianism is just another species of consumerism.

Egalitarians do emphasize resources which satisfy needs and really promote wellbeing, and do reject the upper classes' myth of the happy pauper (would *they* be poor?). But nothing in egalitarianism endorses the mere desire for more things. On the contrary, it treats this desire primarily as a conception of individual wellbeing on which people might disagree. Its main priority is not to resolve such disagreements but to provide the conditions under which individuals can decide these things for themselves. Since at the same time it seeks to satisfy people's needs for respect, community, self-development, personal choice and self-government, it can hardly be accused of materialism!

3

Mutual Respect

Every human being is entitled to our respect. This fundamental moral principle is officially recognized by many political outlooks, but it is especially central to egalitarianism, as well as being the second of its three basic grounds. What is respect, and what does it imply? Philosophers have struggled with these issues for centuries, and will doubtless continue to do so. Although this chapter includes a brief discussion of the philosophical idea of respect, its main aim is to show that even some very ordinary and uncontroversial kinds of respect provide strong arguments for equality. In general, these arguments operate in two ways. First of all, each particular form of respect gives direct support to certain kinds of equality. But each also requires certain conditions of equality if it's to be widely practised, and so provides an indirect argument for those equalities, too.

Fair-mindedness

If you think that mothers should stay at home with their children, then you owe it to mothers to provide a good reason for your opinion. And if you think that the case is different for fathers, then you owe it to both kinds of parents to explain why the difference between them matters. These requirements of moral justification and consistency are part of what's involved in holding any moral opinions at all. They are standards of rational belief, the basic elements of fair-mindedness. They represent a very simple form of respect for others.

Fair-mindedness applies most directly to various forms of discrimination, in which some people are treated worse than others for reasons which obviously don't matter, such as sex or colour or religion. To be sure, white people in Alabama or Cape Town have sometimes thought that they had strong moral arguments for making black people use separate restaurants or toilets, incredible as it seems. But the very power structures which these 'arguments' have been used to support protected them against obvious criticisms. How can you possibly be sure that you do have good reasons for your treatment of others, if they don't even have the right to object? Thus, even the simple respect of fair-mindedness is dependent on a certain equality of power.

Degradation

Another completely uncontroversial kind of respect prohibits treating people in degrading ways. There is no such thing as justified degradation, no moral excuse for failing to respect a person's basic human dignity. As with need, what counts as degradation is to some extent open to argument, depending on your idea of basic decency. For instance, you'd want to argue with a man who considers it an assault on his dignity to have his wife earning higher pay. But there's no doubt that being tortured or raped, or having to beg for food, are degrading and demand urgent redress. More generally, it's obvious that extremes of poverty, powerlessness and persecution are both degrading in themselves and lead to other kinds of degradation.

What's the relation between degradation and equality? The claim that everyone should be secure from degrading treatment and circumstances is itself an egalitarian claim in a world in which so many are not. But to implement this principle may require more far-reaching equalities than it seems. Rape, for instance, is undoubtedly a consequence of the systematic inequalities between men and women and cannot be dissociated from them. Torture and poverty are intimately connected with inequalities of power and wealth. Anyone can piously deplore degradation – but the social policies necessary to prevent it may be more radical than they might imagine!

Exploitation

You don't have to be a socialist to realize that some workers are exploited:

> Mrs Thomas works in a launderette from 9 a.m. to 4 p.m. without a break every day except Friday and Sunday. Her work includes opening up and closing the shop, cleaning it, carrying out service washes and supervising the machines. Her reward is a weekly pay packet of just £18.00. . . . She pays out £3.50 a week for a small flat set above the launderette. At first a job with a home seemed an advantage to Mrs Thomas but now it is a major obstacle to improving her pay. . . . Simply by trying to negotiate a decent rate of pay, Mrs Thomas could face losing both her job and her home.

The central feature of such exploitation is that the employer is taking advantage of the worker's vulnerable situation to extract as much work from her as possible while leaving her barely enough to survive. It's a case of differential *power* being used to gain differential *income* – which of course perpetuates the power relation itself. In his writings on capitalism, Marx argued that the relationship between the capitalist class and the working class is of just this kind. Capitalists take advantage of the fact that without employment, workers would simply starve. They use that advantage to extract as much work as they can, leaving workers with only their subsistence needs catered for. You might disagree that all workers in all capitalist countries are in quite the same position Marx describes, though it would be foolish for anyone to dismiss his views completely. The threat of unemployment certainly forces workers to settle for lower pay than they might otherwise demand, and gives the worst employers more scope. But concentrate for a moment on the moral question: what's wrong with exploitation?

Reverting to arguments from the last chapter, exploitation could be criticized for the low level of wellbeing it imposes on workers, sometimes frustrating even their most urgent needs. But its special moral character lies in taking advantage of the weak position of the exploited, and treating them as mere objects to be made use of. Taking advantage of people like that is yet another form of disrespect for others. We can all recognize it as wrong, and its results as unjust.

Exploitation is one form of extortion, an extortion of work. It is more sophisticated than a plundering army or the forcible eviction of peasants. But wherever there are inequalities of power, some kind of extortion is likely to occur. You might think that it can be avoided by placing limits on the use of power. But how can you do that except by giving more power to the powerless? And since the power in question is often economic, the solution will have to involve democratic economic structures as well as greater equality of income and wealth. Only then could we be reasonably confident that no one was vulnerable enough to be exploited, nor anyone strong enough to exploit others.

The Philosophers' Idea of Respect

Not surprisingly, some philosophers take 'respect for persons' very seriously. Followers of the eighteenth-century philosopher Immanuel Kant have even claimed that this idea is not just an important part of morality, but the ultimate basis for all moral thinking. And some egalitarian philosophers have argued that respect is the ultimate basis for equality.

The philosophical treatment of respect usually starts with the idea that everyone *is* equal in certain special ways. For instance, everyone has needs and abilities, even though needs and abilities vary: the equality lies simply in having them at all. Sometimes the claim is more specific: that everyone has the capacity to be moral, or to be self-directing. The philosopher then argues that because of this fundamental equality, people owe each other a certain fundamental respect. Sometimes it's put like this: once you recognize that others are the same as you in these basic ways, you see that there is only one appropriate attitude you can have towards them, namely one of respect. Or it might be argued this way: anything that has these special characteristics has to be something of real moral worth, and as such commands our respect. Since everyone is equal in the special ways described, it follows that their moral worth is also equal, and thus that the respect due to them must be equal, too.

From there on, the egalitarian argument is that you aren't really showing equal respect for persons unless you treat them in at least broadly egalitarian ways. That would include, of course, being fair-minded, opposing degradation, and rejecting exploitation, but it would extend further. How could you respect someone except by promoting her or his freedom and wellbeing? And so, how could you respect people equally except by promoting equal rights, powers, income, and wealth? Respect is thus. seen as a direct line to a full egalitarian programme.

It's not my intention to criticize these arguments here. They may be a valuable way to systematize and underpin egalitarian views. But they are far too speculative and contentious to carry much weight in the everyday arguments to which this book is addressed, and they belong to a style of argument with which I have little sympathy. For anyone who wants to pursue them, there are some titles in 'References and Further Reading'; the reasons for my lack of sympathy are given in Chapter 10.

Social Superiority

There is yet another common way of showing someone lack of respect, and that's to adopt an attitude of superiority. At their most cutting, attitudes of superiority are attitudes of contempt, disdain, and scorn; their charitable face is shown by patronizing attitudes and condescension; their arrogance is exhibited in snobbery, self-importance, and elitism. Such attitudes are of course rife in inegalitarian societies, and it is a perfectly natural and respectable reaction simply to reject them out of hand on the general principle of equal respect for all. But a reaction is not an argument.

Suppose we accept, for the moment, that attitudes of superiority are sometimes right. That's not enough to justify the specific pattern of superior attitudes found in our own society, where some people feel superior to others because of their *social position*. In our society, being male or female, black or white, rich or poor, powerful or weak, all contribute to your particular social status, your particular place in the hierarchy of prestige. The egalitarian alternative to this pecking order is sometimes called social equality, sometimes equality of status. It is based on the argument that even if attitudes of superiority are sometimes justified, mere social position is never a good enough reason for them.

One kind of superior attitude, found in racists and sexists, is blatantly wrong – it's a bias for which even the most sophisticated rationalization is a transparent failure. The most common rationalization – that white people, or men, are on *average* more intelligent or hard-working or friendly than black people or women – would be irrelevant even if it were true. It would not prove that the racist or sexist is *himself* more intelligent, energetic, or friendly than every woman or every black person. In fact, his belief that it does is self-refuting!

A more sophisticated pattern of superior attitudes in our society is of people with greater wealth and power who disdain and patronize those with less. But mere lack of money and influence doesn't itself make someone worthy of contempt: if people are ever contemptible at all, it is for what they *are*, not for what they *have*. Contempt has to be justified by a lack of personal worth, not wealth. That's what makes these attitudes matters of respect in the first place.

And so the rich and powerful always tend to back up their scorn and snobbery with the myth that the weak and poor aren't where they are by accident, but because of their own inferiority. In other times, other cultures, this inferiority was supposed to be a matter of birth – they were from lower stock, and that was enough to justify the whole social structure. Nowadays, no one is ready to defend quite that rationalization, so we needn't consider it here. Instead, they propound a similar but more sophisticated theory: that the pyramid of wealth and power is also a pyramid of intelligence, industry, skill, and culture, some innate, some acquired. It's these superior qualities which justify superior attitudes: wealth and power are merely their effects.

One of the weaknesses of this rationalization is that its central contention is at best false. At best, because the ideas of intelligence, industry, skill, and culture are all contentious and ambiguous: who is the more intelligent, an electrician who can't understand economics or an economics professor who can't understand wiring? Who's the more skilled? But even if we leave aside such questions, and try to use these terms as uncontroversially as possible, it's obvious that people with the same intelligence, skill, perseverance, and culture can end up in markedly different places on the social heap, for instance if one becomes a primary school teacher and the other a stockbroker. In fact, even the most enthusiastic attempts to explain income distribution in terms of observable personal characteristics like IQ, education and even family background have admitted that these account for less than half the explanation of economic inequality. For the rest of the explanation, they rely partly on 'drive' and 'determination' (which they call the 'D-Factor' to make it sound scientific), and partly on plain old luck.

Even if the rich and powerful *were* more intelligent, etcetera, their airs of superiority would be groundless for at least three reasons. First of all, there are many other forms of superiority. No one could suggest that the privileged have a monopoly on kindness, or courage, or loyalty, or resilience. Whatever your list of the really valuable personal character-istics, you have to admit that they don't all match up with wealth and power.

The second reason is that superiorities of intelligence, industry, skill, and culture are sustained and reinforced by privilege. Privilege can buy more stimulating surroundings, more training, higher motivation, more high culture, more travel, more free time. If, as the rest of this book argues, inequalities of wealth and power are unjustified, then any superiorities which they have been used to acquire are ill-gotten gains. How dare anyone feel smug about them?

The third reason applies to some extent to all attitudes of superiority. However much we might feel like taking credit for our winning qualities, we all know that these are never entirely of our own making. You don't have to believe that 'everything is determined by circumstances' (or even to know what it means!) to recognize the influence of families, neighbourhoods, and schools, or of class, religion, and culture, on the development of personality and ability. No one should feel too comfortable about looking down on others: 'there, but for fortune, go you or I'.

Of course, no one can legislate against superior attitudes. It might even be argued that in small amounts they provide a little harmless colour. But that's a long way from the pervasive, structured, oppressive attitudes which are created and sustained by the central, public inequalities of wealth, power, and title. Those attitudes are insupportable – their remedy, an egalitarian society.

Other Kinds of Respect

Respect crops up in lots of different places not mentioned so far. For instance, in a workgroup or club it may take time to earn what we call the respect of other members. A very wise or knowledgeable scholar may be 'highly respected'. Children are told to respect their elders, soldiers their officers, wives their husbands. All these go beyond the forms of respect already discussed, and they imply *inequalities* – between new and old members, good and bad scholars, ages, ranks, and spouses. Is there anything wrong with such inequalities? Or are they compatible with the egalitarian ideal?

Obviously these kinds of respect are sometimes questionable. The 'respect' of wives for husbands, at least in the traditional, one-way sense, implied an innate sexual inferiority which has no basis. The respect of fellow workers might be withheld out of racism or snobbery. Academic hierarchies can breed exploitation and condescension. But it's an open question whether arguments like these can be used to attack *any* inequality of respect. Different egalitarians are likely to have different views. What's yours?

Would Equality Exploit the Talented?

Are the central forms of respect always on the side of equality? This section considers some arguments to the contrary.

Surely sex, ethnicity, religion and so on are sometimes good reasons for treating people differently. In those cases, fair-mindedness supports inequality.

Egalitarians don't deny that sex, ethnicity and so on are sometimes relevant factors. For instance, sex is part of the justification for maternity leave. But the relevance has to be proved. In the case of maternity leave, the fact that women bear children and men don't is obviously relevant; but even here, current legislation reinforces the prejudice that *caring* for children is also confined to women. That's why egalitarians also call for paternity leave, even if it might be on a different basis from the leave given to mothers.

These arguments for treating people differently according to sex, ethnicity or religion are not, however, arguments for inequality. For the aim is not to favour one sex over the other, or one culture, or one religion, but to treat them equally well by taking account of their differences. The contrast between this and any typical case of discrimination is obvious.

An egalitarian society would prevent talented people from earning high salaries, and force them to work for the benefit of others. That's exploitation of the talented.

The whole essence of exploitation is the use of an inequality of power to achieve further inequalities. It would certainly exploit or take advantage of talented people to use power over them to feather one's own nest while they slept in the cold. (Example: the exploitation of talented singers by unscrupulous managers.) But in an egalitarian society, no one would *take advantage* of the talented. They wouldn't be denied any of the benefits enjoyed by others. No one could call that exploitation, or deny that it showed respect for people with talent. For criticisms of the arguments in favour of talented people getting high incomes, see Chapters 6 to 8.

It's wrong to say that Mrs Thomas (see page 25) is exploited. After all, it was her own choice to take that launderette job. She made a free contract, and benefited from doing so. Far from treating her with disrespect, her employer has done her a favour.

It's true that both parties in a bargain like this usually end up better off as a result of the deal. But how much each benefits, and where each ends up, depend on where they started from. Mrs Thomas may be better off than if she had no job and nowhere to live; but the very fact that her only alternative was unemployment and homelessness gave her employer a power-ful weapon which it was easy to use. That use of power lies at the heart of exploitation.

Sometimes people don't deserve to be respected, because they are so vicious or obnoxious or incompetent. Sometimes they really do deserve contempt.

It's plausible to suggest that people who refuse to respect others deserve the same treatment in return. Perhaps they do; but it's equally plausible to hold that by treating them badly you only diminish yourself. Can anyone with a deep general commitment against degradation, exploitation, and snobbery really act in those ways towards others, or do they have to respect even the wicked out of a sense of common humanity?

Whatever the answer to that question, it has little bearing on the argument of this chapter. That argument has been against the layers of contempt found in our society and created by its hierarchies of power and wealth. The argument has been put without talking about what people 'deserve', but could easily have been expressed that way without altering its conclusion. (For a fuller discussion of deserving, see Chapter 6.) So maybe pimps and torturers, fat cat capitalists and bullying bureaucrats *are* contemptible. That doesn't vindicate existing inequalities but undermines them.

4

A Sense of Community

The idea of community is the third basic ground for equality. But it's not an exclusively left-wing ideal. Under the names of brotherhood, sisterhood, and fraternity, of comradeship, fellowship, and solidarity, the ideal of an interdependent group with a common purpose has played a role in many social outlooks. The argument in this chapter is that anyone who takes this ideal seriously is committed to egalitarianism – its anti-egalitarian use is a deception.

The Importance of Common Purposes

What's so good about community? The most obvious answer is that societies with a strong sense of community are liable to be more stable, more productive, easier to defend. Community is good because it has good effects for 'society as a whole'. These effects explain the attraction of community from all social points of view – a sense of common purpose confers order, prosperity, and strength on a feudal monarchy as much as on a socialist democracy.

But community has another value: it satisfies what everyone recognizes as a common human need. Practically everyone needs a certain sense of belonging: not complete immersion in a group, but a feeling that its members are tied together by something more than mere self-interest. How important you take this need to be depends very much on your conception of human wellbeing, and whether you are attracted or repelled by the vision of rugged individualism associated so strongly with American culture. But even the most individualistic characters in the American imagination have some communal ties: think of the family and corporate loyalties in *Dallas* and *Dynasty*. There's a close connection here with the need for an identity, since the groups you belong to help to give you a sense of who you are. From this angle, too, community is of interest to a variety of social outlooks, but especially to egalitarianism with its explicit commitment on needs.

For many people, the value of community runs deeper than either of these answers. For them, common purposes are important not just to serve the needs of individuals, nor simply to generate social benefits, but because there's something admirable about community for its own sake. A sense of community is not just a means to other ends, but an end in itself. And why shouldn't social cohesion be given as much value in its own right as the stability, prosperity, and strength it promotes?

These questions about the value of common purposes aren't intended to be decisive. In our culture, people disagree on the value they attach to community, and it is unlikely that argument alone is enough to change their views. This chapter is addressed to people who do care about community. What should they think about equality?

The Link between Community and Equality

A sense of community strengthens and extends the support for the principles of equality in many ways. Here are some of the most central and important.

Community and wellbeing

The argument of Chapter 2 rested on the fact that even common decency involves some concern for the wellbeing of others: enough, at least, to justify providing the minimal material and institutional requirements for a satisfying life. The ideal of community supports this concern in another way. For without a shared feeling of personal security and basic wellbeing, how can a society hope to sustain any real sense of community? How could neglecting the basic needs and wellbeing of a section of society result in anything but their resentment and alienation?

A sense of community also acts as a more positive force. When you treat people as your brothers, sisters, or comrades, you show a stronger concern for their wellbeing than what's required by decency. You're prepared to make sacrifices for them – though you also expect the same in return. So community supports a more generous attitude towards universal wellbeing than the idea of need on its own.

Community and respect

Of course there can be no genuine sense of community between degrader and degraded, or exploiter and exploited – these relationships mock the very idea of community. But solidarity is also incompatible with attitudes of superiority, because they distance people from each other, create barriers and reinforce divisions. A sense of community only thrives when people's attitudes towards each other go beyond minimal respect to the respect of social equals.

Community and economics

It's a truism that substantial differences in income, wealth, and economic power create differences in lifestyle, outlook, and values. That's why social classes, though formed by the economy, have different cultures, too. By contrast, a sense of community depends on a common culture, with a core of shared attitudes and values. Economic equality is thus a basic precondition for a developed sense of community.

Once established, a sense of community helps to sustain the economic equality it depends on. For any economy involves relations of exchange or 'reciprocity' – you scratch my back and I'll scratch yours. Our present economy conducts this exchange very narrowly, trading goods and services for specific payments in return. Since a sense of community embodies mutual concern and respect, and a sense of shared problems and aims, it naturally supports a different and deeper form of reciprocity: people are more generous in their day to day relationships, and they get in return not a specific benefit but the general generosity of others.

A good modern example of this relationship at work is the British system of blood donation. Unlike many other countries, donors aren't paid for their blood; what they get in return is the knowledge that other people's blood will be available if they need it. As the example shows, this generalized reciprocity transfers resources from people who have more than they need to people who have less. So it tends towards greater economic equality.

Community and politics

In organizations marked by power struggles and personal animosities, community is at best an aspiration, and often mere rhetoric: the use of terms like 'comrade' and 'sister' can sound like a sick joke. But politics can provide some striking experiences of fellowship – within a residents' association or a local political party, or on a larger scale at a public rally or in support of a cause. These examples illustrate how community and political equality go hand in hand, since such groups only sustain their sense of community if everyone feels involved in the decisions being taken and leaders are seen to be accountable to their supporters. They also show that although community depends on a shared purpose, it doesn't mean mindless conformity: anyone who has ever been involved in such a group knows that they can have plenty of internal disagreements and debates. What matters is that these take place within a framework of common concern and mutual respect.

Community and discrimination

Sexual, racial, ethnic, or religious inequality sometimes strengthens the cohesion of oppressed groups, but of course it hardens social divisions. Its whole thrust is to deny that discriminator and victim have anything in common. It is the antithesis of community.

Degrees of community

It would be unrealistic, and is in any case unnecessary, to expect our society to become one big happy family, with everyone caring as much about strangers as about their nearest and dearest. That's not what egalitarians are looking for. There are degrees of community, ranging from selfish individualism at one extreme to total social commitment at the other, and these correspond to degrees of equality. As a sense of community increases, so does the extent to which a group pays attention to its members' needs, dignity, and aspirations. More community and more equality go hand in hand.

Is Equality Divisive?

Anti-egalitarians deny these links between community and equality. Here are some typical objections.

Equality is itself divisive. For egalitarianism attacks the privileged, and seeks to benefit the unprivileged. As a result, it sets women against men, black people against white, the poor against the rich. It destroys communities, and puts strife in their place.

This charge is mistaken. Egalitarianism didn't create social divisions – they were there, with their conspicuous contrasts of wealth, power, and status, long before egalitarianism poked its nose into things. To question these divisions is to stand for community, not against it.

But a stable hierarchy, even if it is in a sense 'divided', can still have a sense of community. For just as family life assigns unequal roles to parents and children, and education to teachers and pupils, so too can a community have unequal roles. Egalitarians may not like these communities, but they can hardly deny their existence.

Let's consider these 'hierarchical communities' more closely. Like any hierarchy of power, wealth, and status, they can generate some subversive ideas – that the people at the top aren't too wildly concerned about the people at the bottom, that they don't have much respect for them, that they put a lot less effort into keeping the system going and take a lot more out of it, and that, however cosy things become, you'd better not forget who's boss. These ideas don't do much to sustain a sense of fellowship, and must therefore be suppressed. But to suppress *true* ideas is a deceit, and any resulting sense of community is a cruel deception. Could these ideas be anything *but* true? Have you ever been part of a hierarchy in which they weren't?

As for the parent/child and teacher/pupil relationships, the degree of inequality can be overrated. There is certainly a mutual commitment to wellbeing, and a rejection of attitudes of superiority: parents and teachers are obviously in some ways expected to be more competent and knowledgeable than their children and pupils, but it would be ridiculous for them to feel superior about it! These relationships are also marked by mutual obligation – each side has different duties, but they are arguably equally balanced. In fact, you could hardly find better examples of generalized reciprocity. The only problem for egalitarianism is that the authority asserted by parents over children and teachers over pupils is exercised without *consent* – it is, as they say, 'paternalistic'. Maybe that kind of inequality is sometimes compatible with community, so long, of course, as it doesn't rest on deceit. For instance, it makes sense with young children. But once you become an adult offspring or student, paternalistic authority surely *does* rest on a falsehood: the falsehood that you haven't really grown up, or that you are incapable of appreciating the grounds for a curriculum or teaching regime. The moral of the story is that community, inequality, and truth don't mix.

The ideal of community is fine for certain kinds of groups organized around particular purposes, but it's strictly limited in scope. Humanity in general, whole countries, even whole cities are too big and diverse for a sense of common purpose.

There are certainly examples of broad unity of purpose in whole nations, particularly in times of national emergency. The widespread nostalgia which is felt, for instance, for this aspect of wartime Britain suggests that country-wide solidarity is both possible and valued. Within unequal societies, it takes something like a war (a 'great leveller') to establish this feeling; arguably, a more equal society could sustain solidarity on a more permanent basis. At the very least, it's reasonable to believe that a whole society could have some elements of a sense of community, and could design certain institutions, such as its health service and system of education, with communitarian ideals in mind.

But it's probably true that a sense of community is easier to sustain in smaller groups than in larger ones. That's not an argument against equality, but is rather in favour of encouraging small groups in which both community and equality can thrive. It means, for instance, decentralizing power so that small groups can take important decisions, extending local and industrial democracy so that neighbourhoods and workgroups aren't just told what to do by managers and bureaucrats, and providing the resources necessary for full participation. These measures may not of themselves bring about greater equality in society as a whole, but they would foster equality within each group. This is of course related to the question of scope discussed in Chapter 1.

Solidarity within a group may weaken solidarity between groups. It thrives on conflict, and on treating members of the group better than non-members. So it actually reinforces inequality.

It is important to remember that arguments based on community only supplement the other arguments for equality. Those other arguments already apply to the treatment of one group by another, just as they apply to individuals. Community reinforces and extends the arguments for equality within groups, but it doesn't override arguments for equality between them. Of course groups sometimes feel like doing other groups down, just as individuals do. But neither groups nor individuals *have* to act that way. The sense of community you enjoy in belonging to, say, a cycling club doesn't have to do down people who aren't interested in bikes; one nation's pride doesn't have to conflict with another's. If the scope for community is limited, then the case it provides for more extensive equality is limited, too. But that doesn't give groups a free hand to do whatever they like.

PART TWO
Equality or Inequality?

5

Is Equality of Opportunity Enough?

Here's one kind of equality which everyone in our society seems to agree with. And for a lot of people, it seems to be just the right compromise – to be the kind of equality which leaves people free to move ahead of the pack if they want to. But the appearance of consensus can't be trusted – equality of opportunity means different things to different people. There are at least five forms of equal opportunity currently in fashion, and all of them have serious limitations. Egalitarians ought to be interested in something very different.

Which Equality of Opportunity?

So you believe in equality of opportunity – but which kind do you mean? Here are the five most common versions, with a brief account of their attractions.

'Careers open to talents'

Originally formulated in the period of the French Revolution, this principle called for high public offices to be opened to anyone able to fill them, not just the nobility. The general extension of the principle is that jobs and educational places should be filled on merit alone. Though widely proclaimed, it's still considered in practice to apply more strongly to public sector jobs than to private business. For instance, laws against discrimination by sex and colour apply to all employers, but only public employers are supposed to ignore family connections and friendship.

'Fair equal opportunity'

This idea goes by many names. It stems from realizing that 'careers open to talents' still operates to the benefit of people with well-heeled parents. These people have a better chance of developing their talents than other people with the same basic abilities. The aim of 'fair equal opportunity' is to make sure that people with the same abilities and aspirations are treated the same from the start. Then, later on, awarding education and jobs according to merit won't be unfair.

'Affirmative action'

Also called positive action, this principle aims to give positive support to members of groups which have been discriminated against in the past, notably women and black people. In its standard form, employers and administrators still have to fill jobs and educational places on the basis of merit. But they are expected to encourage applications from well-qualified women and black people by appropriate advertising, carefully designed training programmes, and an explicit rejection of discriminatory practices. Whether they've succeeded is judged by whether the proportion of women and black people at each level of employment or training corresponds to the proportions available in the surrounding population, but these 'targets' are not compulsory, and aren't supposed to conflict with deciding on merit alone.

One of the strongest justifications of affirmative action is that compared to white males, women and black people are disadvantaged while growing up. They face special obstacles and tend to receive less encouragement and attention. So to give them some special attention later is only righting the balance. A related argument is that for true equality of opportunity, young women and black people need to be assured that it's worth their while to apply for places and jobs. Finally, affirmative action can be seen as a public expression to all women and black people of a determination not to be associated with past injustices.

'Reverse discrimination'

Although affirmative action is meant to help women and minorities to get better jobs and education, it retains the basic idea of deciding on 'merit' alone. A policy of 'reverse' or 'positive' or 'compensatory' discrimination goes one step further, and requires employers and educators to give positive preference to these groups. The main arguments for reverse discrimination are the same as for affirmative action, but they take a broader view of the kind of remedy necessary to correct for past injustice. A mere intention not to discriminate may not be enough to ensure that women and black people are actually offered education and jobs, because they may have been prevented at an earlier stage from gaining necessary qualifications. Affirmative action can also be very slow, and its use of targets has a tendency in practice to encourage reverse discrimination anyway. So why not admit what you're doing? Proponents of reverse discrimination also emphasize the importance of 'role models' in high-status jobs, and argue that these can only be ensured by reverse discrimination in the first generation. Another argument is that it's good for society as a whole for there to be more women and black people in positions of power and status, and that this boosts the self-esteem of other members of these groups, too.

'Proportional equal opportunity'

Reverse discrimination doesn't say *how much* preference women and black people should get. 'Proportional equal opportunity' is a kind of quota system which insists that the proportions of women and black people in each kind of job or education should mirror the proportion of women and black people in society as a whole. One possible source of this idea is simply that it's the most natural explanation of what racial and sexual equality *are* – women and men, and black people and white, being on average equally well-off. One of the main arguments in its favour is to point out that if black people and women weren't being discriminated against then they'd be proportionally represented without any need for quotas. But because it's so difficult to prove discrimination in practice, and because there's so much resistance to reform, quotas are the only practical way of dealing with the problem.

An Equal Opportunity – to be Unequal!

These five standard forms of equality of opportunity have one thing in common. They all take it for granted that there is a system of jobs and forms of education which vary in pay and prospects, and that more people want the good ones than can have them. The whole point of these principles is to regulate the competition for advantage. All that differs is who ends up on top – people from privileged backgrounds, or people with the best natural talents, or a representative sample of talented men and women, black and white. The choice between them decides who will benefit from inequalities but doesn't change the inequalities themselves. Of course, this gives certain types of people a good reason to prefer one form of equal opportunity to the others. For instance, it gives talented white men a reason for preferring careers open to talents, and talented black women a reason to prefer quotas. But are there any good reasons to accept any of these principles? Should we care about how inequalities are handed round, or only about how to get rid of them?

The biggest problem is that principles of equal opportunity help to make systems of inequality seem reasonable and acceptable. They shift the whole issue away from whether inequalities of wealth, power, status, and education are themselves justifiable, to the question of how to distribute these inequalities. The implication is that as long as the competition for advantage is fair, advantage itself is beyond criticism. The winners feel entitled to their winnings and the losers blame themselves.

Equality of opportunity in its standard forms also undermines a sense of community. It encourages people to concentrate on their own individual prospects. Their talents are likely to separate them from the people they grew up with; the system as a whole puts them into competition with everyone else from the moment they're born. The only kind of solidarity likely to emerge from this process is a certain arrogant *esprit de corps* of the successful and a shared depression among the unsuccessful. Neither is of much value in itself, nor is either likely to advance egalitarian aims.

Even in its own terms, equality of opportunity faces a very serious problem. How can you give children equal opportunities if their parents have completely unequal resources?

Do you take children out of families altogether? If you do, where do you put them? And if you don't, won't the children of the rich and powerful inevitably have better chances in life than those of the poor and weak? Equality of opportunity pretends that the successes and failures of one generation can be separated from the life-chances of the next. But that, of course, is impossible.

Is There Anything Good About It?

There are a few benefits of equal opportunity, particularly the stronger kinds, but it's always a case of mixed blessings. First of all, it *is* likely that having more women and black people in positions of power will have some impact on sexist and racist attitudes throughout society, and therefore on the status of women and black people in general. For instance, a man must find it harder to adopt an air of superiority towards women in general if he's constantly reminded that some women are better off than he is. And the success of some women gives other women greater self-confidence and self-esteem. Since sexist and racist attitudes and the inequality of status which they express are particularly entrenched and obnoxious, any contribution equal opportunity can make towards overturning them has got to be welcomed. But the gain has to be set against the degree to which equal opportunity strengthens other, meritocratic attitudes of superiority and inadequacy.

Another effect of equal opportunity is that in the end it can help mend certain kinds of social division. If black people become on average as well off as white people, then society is going to be less divided along racial lines. Black people won't be so disaffected as a group; white people won't be so arrogant. Of course, in its initial stages an equal opportunity programme can increase hostility, as white males fight to retain their privileges. But that division was already there, and equal opportunity may be a more satisfactory way of dealing with it than, say, fighting in the streets. The cohesive effect of equality of opportunity isn't perfect, though, since it also strengthens individualistic competition and perpetuates divisions between the successful and the unsuccessful.

It might also be argued that although equal opportunity has no direct effect on economic inequality, it could have an indirect effect. There are several ways of trying to show this, though all of them are open to question. First of all, you might argue that the new 'winners' from disadvantaged groups will help other members who lose. But will they? Mightn't they use their positions and abilities to benefit themselves still more? Wouldn't they have been more use to the disadvantaged as talented leaders among them than as people who escaped? It's also an interesting fact that even the more radical kinds of equal opportunity are rarely expressed in terms of class background. The tendency will be for the women and black people who benefit to come mainly from better-off families. Will they really use their new advantages to promote other kinds of equality?

A second way of making the case for an indirect effect on inequality is to argue that certain jobs and other social roles now have bad pay, conditions, and status *because* they are occupied only by women or black people. Typical examples are cleaning, laundry work, hairdressing, and housework, all of which are done primarily by women. If men had to do these things, they would become both more esteemed and better paid. The argument is certainly plausible, but obviously limited in scope. If it's right, we should expect equal opportunity to improve the jobs now done by women and black people, but to have little effect on whatever inequalities already exist among white men. In Britain, for instance, hairdressers earn about half as much as plasterers – equal opportunity might do away with that gap. But plasterers earn less than half as much as university teachers. Since both occupations are dominated by white males, equal opportunity couldn't be expected to affect the gap between *them* very much, nor between a plasterer and a millionaire property developer for whom she worked.

You might respond to this point with a third argument: that the gap between the property developer and the plasterer is sustained, in part, by racial and sexual divisions among workers. Equal opportunity would bring greater unity to the working class as a whole, which would then be in a better position to act to change the system. Maybe there's something in this argument, though maybe not, since equal opportunity strengthens other divisions, such as between 'skilled' and 'unskilled' work. But in either case, you've moved from issues of basic principles to questions of tactics. The argument no longer considers equal opportunity as valuable for its own sake, nor even for making a positive contribution to other equalities. It merely removes one of many practical obstacles to building a truly egalitarian political movement.

There is, however, a final point in favour of equality of opportunity itself. It does, after all, extend opportunities to a wider range of people. Admittedly, its main effect is for some women and black people to do better only by some white men doing worse. But white men don't lose the opportunity to do well, they merely have slightly reduced chances. You might ask what good there is in an opportunity to do well if you don't succeed, and the answer has to be that there's not a lot. It may even be worse than having no opportunity to begin with, since opportunities give rise to frustrated expectations and self-reproach. But on the whole, people seem to prefer having even a slim, loaded chance of doing well to having no chance at all. Yet the extension of opportunity also has its cost. People who might otherwise have contributed to a common struggle for equality scramble to the top on the equal-opportunity ladder, or are simply too busy trying to climb it to have any time left over.

These arguments give some support to the widespread idea that if inequalities must exist, they should at least be regulated by some kind of equal opportunity. But they do nothing for the belief that equality of opportunity is the only kind of equality worth caring about. How could they, when each of them depends on values which equal opportunity on its own helps to frustrate?

One more thing is often said in favour of equality of opportunity – that it allows more scope for people to make use of their individual capacities, since education and jobs are filled according to ability. There may be some truth in this, but not very much. For equality of opportunity doesn't really match up positions to abilities – it gives the *best* positions to the *most* able. A lot of other able people can end up with training and jobs which hardly develop their capacities at all. But this supposed defence of equal opportunity does suggest a different, truly egalitarian idea.

An Egalitarian View

The truly egalitarian attitude towards opportunity is to give everyone the means to develop their capacities in a satisfying and fulfilling way. That can't be achieved by competing for the jobs and training we have at the moment – it requires a restructuring which really does try to match social roles to individual capacities. Boring, tedious jobs which don't foster self-development have to be attacked, by technological means, by sharing their tasks out in a different way, by job rotation, or at least by drastically limiting their working hours. Truly egalitarian opportunity is revolutionary.

The opportunity to develop one's capacities in a fulfilling way is sometimes called a higher need. In any event, it is obviously an important element of wellbeing, which you'd need a very good reason to suppress. Certainly, a society which denies some people the genuine opportunity to develop their capacities is adding insult to injury if it despises them for their shallowness as well. By contrast, any society with a strong sense of community would clearly have a strong positive commitment to the egalitarian principle of opportunity. That principle would require a much greater economic equality than we now have, particularly in production. And its determined opposition to racism and sexism would completely outdistance the less radical principles discussed earlier. No wonder it's not the kind of 'equal opportunity' the modern consensus defends!

Fairness in the Game of Life

People sometimes react very strongly to criticisms of equal opportunity. Here are some typical examples.

Even if the standard forms of equal opportunity don't go very far, they're surely much better than nothing. Better than apartheid, for instance.

No one's denied that. The argument has only been that they aren't all they're cracked up to be, and that they'd be surpassed in a truly egalitarian society.

But at least equal opportunity makes the competition for inequality fair.

In self-contained, specialized competitions like flower shows and chess tournaments, we have a good idea of what counts as fair play: the competitors enter under the same conditions, are afforded the same facilities, are judged by the same standards, and everything is set up to reward what everyone agrees on as excellence. But what's fairness in the Game of Life? Is it fair for people to have different innate abilities? And if it is, why isn't it fair for them to have different family influences, or to make use of their family connections? What qualities is the Game of Life *supposed* to reward? Why should we think of it as a tournament, as opposed to, say, a lottery?

The 'fairness' argument for equal opportunity relies on comparing life to a competitive game. That comparison is not just morally repellent, it's also too loose to justify any specific form of equal opportunity. Only if you already have a notion about the sorts of people who *should* win in the Great Human Pentathlon can you begin to specify its rules of play. And that means having some good arguments for inequality in the first place. In this way, also, equality of opportunity is intimately connected with a belief in other inequalities.

The standard forms of equal opportunity do favour other equalities, because they mean more skilled people are in the market for skilled jobs. Being in greater supply, doctors, lawyers, managers, and so on aren't able to charge so much for their services. It's a simple question of supply and demand.

This objection has some validity, but depends a lot on circumstances. The 'market for skilled jobs' is not a system of perfect competition in our society or any other, notoriously so for doctors and lawyers! On the contrary, a greater supply of educated people often leads simply to raising the level of qualifications which a job supposedly requires. But in some conditions more equality of opportunity in one of its standard forms could produce more equal incomes. This doesn't remove the basic difference between principles which regulate the competition for advantages, and principles opposed to these advantages themselves.

Reverse discrimination and quotas are in fact much worse than fair equality of opportunity, because the only good reason for offering education or jobs is the ability to do them. Everything else is irrelevant. In fact, that's what makes sexual and racial discrimination wrong to begin with!

Why *should* ability be the only reason for making an appointment? After all, you know that the appointment has a range of effects: on getting a certain job done, of course, but also on racist and sexist attitudes, and on racial and sexual divisions in society. These are important effects, and it would simply be irrational to ignore them. What makes reverse discrimination quite different from the discrimination it replaces is that it aims to eliminate such attitudes and divisions, while racism and sexism aim to perpetuate them.

That being said, it is of course possible for reverse discrimination to produce a racist and sexist backlash which reinforces social divisions, and to favour well-off black people and women at the expense of badly-off white males. It's for these reasons, perhaps, that current legislation tends to adopt the uneasy compromise position of affirmative action. Only a careful examination of particular circumstances can tell whether the risks involved in one form of equal opportunity are better or worse than those of any other.

But reverse discrimination makes white males pay for their fathers' sins, and compensates black people and women for their parents' suffering. It isn't the right adjustment.

To be sure, the past victims of racism and sexism *should* themselves be compensated, and the past oppressors *should* pay. That would be a fair piece of egalitarian justice, all right. But the argument for reverse discrimination is not that the debts of parents should be visited on their children. It is, first of all, that these children are themselves gainers and losers from racism and sexism, and so today's white males do owe compensation to their black and female contemporaries. Secondly, it is that reverse discrimination is necessary for achieving certain effects, such as the provision of role models, a wider range of views in the corridors of power, bolstered self-esteem, and public testimony of the rejection of racism and sexism.

Anyhow, in what sense do young white males 'pay' for reverse discrimination? They do less well than they might have done under, say, fair equality of opportunity; but under that system women and black people do less well than they would under reverse discrimination. In any inegalitarian structure, someone 'pays' for others to do better. It's no worse for white men to do the paying than for someone else to do it.

6

Do Some People Deserve More Than Others?

People will take to the streets on behalf of freedom and equality, but you don't see many demonstrations over what people *deserve*. To many people, that question seems old-fashioned and irrelevant. Even the English language conspires against it: how can you take an idea seriously when its noun form, 'desert', is spelt like an arid wasteland and sounds like ice cream? But in fact the concept of desert is one of the most common ideas in moral discussion, which you can hear practically every day of the week. If that sounds exaggerated, just listen for a few days to what people say and you'll soon change your mind.

A particularly fertile environment for desert is pay differentials. Ask well-paid people to justify their income, and they'll almost always end up saying they deserve it – for the training, the responsibility, the stress, and so on. But to assess the force of such arguments, it helps to look a little at the different ways desert operates. What one finds is that the word 'deserve' is used in a wide variety of cases. Most of these are just as well catered for by other moral concepts, but there seem to be at least two areas in which the idea of desert has its own special role. These can be called 'merit desert' and 'compensation desert'. Once those ideas are clear, it will be possible to separate specific questions of desert from other issues, and to see how weak the case for deserved inequality really is. But since desert won't go away, this chapter concludes by discussing its role in an egalitarian society.

Rewards for Personal Merit

Once when the English cricket team won a test match in India, the *Guardian* said that their captain deserved the victory. In saying that, it was using the idea of merit desert in a common and typical way. The captain had done something good – managed his team well – and was therefore thought to deserve something good in return, namely victory. Judgments of merit desert always start with a prior value judgment, in this case about the captain's management. (Note that the value judgment doesn't have to be a moral one.) The special job done by desert is to use the underlying value judgment to *justify* something, in this case the team's victory.

Merit desert isn't always a case of 'good for good' as in this example. It can also be bad for bad ('criminals deserve to be punished'); even middling for middling ('your exam paper deserves a C'). But in every case someone or something is judged or appraised or evaluated, and some sort of treatment or situation is deemed to be an appropriate response.

There's nothing mysterious about the connection between merit desert and inequality. The whole *point* of merit desert is to transform evaluations of people into differences in the way they're treated, with the good prospering in various ways and the bad suffering. You can't take both merit desert and equality seriously. But egalitarians have a choice. They can attack merit desert head-on, rejecting the whole idea of it. Or they can try to restrict its effects, by denying that it justifies any major differences of income, power, or status. This chapter looks at both strategies, but favours the second.

Compensations for your Pains

If I kick a football through your kitchen window, you deserve to be compensated for the damage I've caused you. You deserve compensation not because there's anything admirable about you, but simply because somebody else has broken your window. Of course, if the two of us had been playing in your garden, if you had told me not to worry about the window, that a football couldn't do any harm, then it would be your own fault if your window got broken and you wouldn't deserve a penny from me.

In general, questions of compensation desert arise when you suffer some loss, harm, or deficiency. Your claim is strengthened if the loss is someone *else's* fault, but it's cancelled if it's your *own* fault. Inevitably, this 'own-fault' clause makes room for a lot of controversy. For instance, if it's well-known that people play football in their gardens and that footballs sometimes go through their neighbours' windows, and if it's easy and common to get yourself insured against such mishaps, then you might well be considered at fault if your window was uninsured. It's not surprising, then, that there are sophisticated systems of legislation and insurance which try to sort out in advance who should be compensated for what.

Compensation itself is quite compatible with equality. If everyone starts off equal, and somebody suffers some loss, then compensation *restores* equality. In fact, without compensation you couldn't possibly maintain equality over time. But the own-fault clause rocks the boat. It means that some losses don't get compensated and so equality isn't maintained. As time goes by, the gap widens between people who mess up their own lives and people who behave prudently.

As with merit desert, egalitarians can try to deal with compensation desert in two different ways. The 'head-on' attack argues that no one can really be blamed for mistakes and losses, and so every loss deserves to be compensated. The 'restricted scope' attack argues that the own-fault clause can only be applied to certain kinds of case, which don't affect any of egalitarianism's central aims.

Five Useful Distinctions

Once desert is unleashed in an argument, it has a tendency to run rampant. So if you want to keep on top of things, it helps to remember a few distinctions. Here are five, each applied to a common anti-egalitarian argument.

1. Desert versus ought

Check that 'deserves' isn't being used simply as another way of saying that someone ought to have something. For instance, in 'Mother always wanted you to have this ring, so you deserve it', the idea of desert isn't doing any special work. The real work is being done by the idea that if a woman owns a ring she has the right to dispose of it by bequest, which is an issue about property rights, not reward or compensation.

Application: In an argument about whether company directors should get huge expense accounts, your companion gradually gives up the idea that they have done anything particularly praiseworthy to deserve them. Suddenly the ground shifts to, 'But the shareholders *agreed* that the directors should have expense accounts, therefore they deserve them.' This isn't a question of desert, but of the property rights of shareholders.

2. Desert versus need

You might well hear people say things like 'Everyone deserves to have enough to eat' or 'Those flood victims deserve our help'. Probably all that's meant is that since people need food and victims need help, they ought to get them. But there are possible connections with the specialized forms of desert. You might argue that people deserve to get what they need because being a person is a very valuable or worthy thing. That's a case of using merit desert to justify the satisfaction of needs. Or you might argue that these particular flood victims deserve help because they can't possibly be blamed for their predicament. That's a point about compensation desert.

Application: In a discussion about whether there should be more state investment in housing, your companion is quite prepared to grant that housing is needed, but won't accept this as a conclusive argument. If you shift to the question, 'But don't you think everyone *deserves* to live in a decent house?', you run the risk of merely repeating yourself. On the other hand, you might make more headway by arguing that many people are homeless due to circumstances beyond their control, such as idiotic government housing policies and mass unemployment. Then you've got a stronger case that they deserve to be compensated.

3. Desert versus entitlement

Issues of desert are often institutionalized by means of competitions, races, examinations, trials, legislation, and insurance. If you think that the best runners deserve to be honoured, it makes sense to set up a procedure both to determine who the best runners are and to say how they should be honoured, for instance a race and a medal. If you think that people who lose their jobs should be compensated, then it makes sense to set up a system for redundancy payments and unemployment benefit.

Once these procedures and systems – these social institutions – are in operation, they *entitle* people who meet certain conditions to certain kinds of treatment. For instance, the person who crosses the finishing line first is entitled to the medal. Then there are *two* justifications for Carl Lewis standing on the winner's platform at the Olympics: he deserves to (because he's so fast), and he's entitled to (because he won the race). In a well-designed institution, the justifications go together – whoever deserves is also entitled. But inevitably there will be some cases where people are entitled to things they don't deserve, or deserve things they're not entitled to, and this distinction can easily get lost in the heat of an argument.

Application: Your companion attacks the whole social welfare system because 'some of those people don't really want to work'. Of course, you may wish to defend people who refuse to do the kind of work which your companion wouldn't touch with a barge pole, but that may not be a very promising approach. An alternative is to admit for the sake of argument that freeloaders do exist, but to point out that this sort of thing is an unavoidable effect of setting up institutions to provide what many people genuinely deserve. Most welfare claimants deserve their benefits; 'scroungers' perhaps don't deserve them, but they're entitled to them given the way the system operates. The onus is on your companion either to deny that *anyone* deserves benefits, or to show that a different system would be better at helping only those who deserve it.

4. Desert versus incentives

Merit desert rewards the good and punishes the bad. But rewards and punishments are also incentives – they motivate people to act in certain ways. It's useful to recognize that desert justifications and incentive justifications have very different structures. Incentive justifications are aimed at *motivation* – they justify rewards in terms of the actions which the offer of rewards will encourage. There's no necessary connection between these incentives and desert, though the two often coincide. For an obvious example, think of people who are utterly dedicated to a cause and make enormous sacrifices for it. They may deserve high praise and recognition, but it would be absurd, even insulting, to think of that praise and recognition as an incentive. They deserve it precisely *because* they act unselfishly, and if you find out later that fame is their real spur you have to conclude that they don't deserve it after all.

But in many situations it's easy to imagine that rewards or penalties are justified by both desert and incentive. For instance, that pupils who work hard both deserve good grades and are motivated by them. The supposed coincidence helps anti-egalitarians, because they can jump back and forth between two different arguments as it suits them. Conversely, to undermine the arguments egalitarians have to stalk down each in turn.

Application: Your companion argues that good students deserve to get a better education than bad ones. You attack the argument, maybe on the ground that, after all, bright kids can't take much credit for their ability – that it's due to heredity and/or environment. Your companion shifts ground and defends the policy as encouraging students to work, thereby helping to maintain educational excellence. Now it's an incentive argument, and before taking on that one it's worth confirming the first point: that, anyway, they don't deserve a better education simply on account of being so clever. Otherwise, when you've defeated the incentive argument, you're likely to witness the dramatic rebirth of the desert argument: 'But surely good students deserve rewards for a job well done . . .'

5. Substantial versus token rewards

If the point of merit desert is not to motivate people, what is it? The most plausible answer is: to express or symbolize the value judgments which merit desert always depends on. The most typical expressions of such value judgments are praise and blame. There are also prizes, medals, rewards, punishments, examination marks, titles, degrees. But none of these things have to be very substantial to do their work. A gold medal doesn't have to be made of gold; an acting award doesn't have to be a million dollars. Expressions of value judgments are, literally, *tokens* of esteem. So one of the handiest kinds of 'restricted scope' arguments against desert is to challenge substantial inequalities with the claim that, as far as desert goes, token inequalities would do just as well.

Application: Does the average doctor deserve an income of £25,000? Well, some of the income might be deserved as a compensation for long hours, responsibility, training – we'll come back to that later. But suppose your companion argues that doctors deserve, say, £10,000 of their differential over dockers just because being a doctor is so much more important and socially useful. The £10,000 is purely a question of merit, society's way of saying 'thanks'. One counter-argument attacks the underlying value judgment: doctors aren't more important than dockers, just different. But even if we accept for the sake of argument that they are, why express this with £10,000? Why not, for instance, simply by the convention of calling doctors 'Dr'? Or by an annual vote of thanks down at the health centre? Either of these serves just as effectively to express our gratitude. The idea that merit has to be recognized via substantial differences of income (or power, or status) simply doesn't hold water.

A Frontal Assault on the Whole Idea

Desert is vulnerable to two head-on attacks, to do with responsibility and with value judgments. Even if they aren't completely convincing, they do provide grounds for a 'restricted scope' view of desert.

Responsibility

Both merit and compensation desert are threatened by controversy over how far people are really responsible for their actions. Compensation is denied to people whose losses and disabilities are their own fault, but can people really be held responsible for their mistakes? After all, their ability to choose is determined by their genetic make-up, their upbringing, the influences of culture and friends, and so on. The individuals who make choices are at the end of whole networks of causes stretching out in a million different directions – why should *they* have to carry the can?

There's a similar point for merit desert. You may be brainy or good-looking or creative, and these are valued qualities, but can you really take any credit for them? Maybe you were born that way; maybe you went to good schools; maybe you were pushed by your parents. Why should you benefit, when you're only what you are due to circumstances?

The general argument is that no one is really responsible for their actions, so desert can never get a foothold. Its main problem is that the basic premise is so contentious. Is responsibility really an illusion? And if it were, what would become of the value we give to freedom and self-determination? There must surely be something right in the idea that people can choose how to act and can be held responsible for their choices. These are difficult philosophical issues which, as usual, take us out of the stream of everyday political argument and so away from the concerns of this book.

But even if you reject the wholesale attack on responsibility, it still has a point. At the very least, it shows that claims of responsibility have to be much more modest than people generally make them. So much of what people achieve is a matter of being in the right place at the right time, of having good luck in family, teachers, friends, and circumstances, that no one is in a strong position to take *much* credit for the way their lives turn out. There's no such thing as a literally self-made man. And so any judgment of desert will have to look closely at where responsibility really lies.

Value judgments

Merit desert always starts with a value judgment. But value judgments are notoriously contentious. You may think that Severiano Ballesteros is an excellent golfer, while I rank him rather low because of his unorthodox style. Maybe you think highly of Frank Sinatra for his singing and I think little of him for his politics. How can opinions which are so open to dispute be the basis for anything?

Again, the wholesale version of this attack – that all value judgments are inherently subjective or unjustifiable or disputable – is a philosophical thesis which is itself open to question. Certainly, this whole book is written on the assumption that it isn't entirely true. But even if it's wrong, it has elements of truth. In particular, it's a reminder that the value judgment underlying a claim of merit desert is always open to scrutiny.

Suppose you think that Barry Manilow deserves his wealth for being such a popular entertainer. One way I can challenge that is to deny the value judgment: what's so good about being popular? Popularity may only be a sign that the general public are suckers. Alternatively, I can admit the value judgment, but set other value judgments against it: for instance, that it's good to be popular, but it's more important to have a lovely voice. And only singers with good voices are really deserving.

Speaking generally, the value judgments underlying common claims of desert are often open to these two kinds of objection, and so fail to provide a proper basis for desert. That's not to deny the possibility of valid value judgments, but only to recognize the difficulties of making them. Some of the arguments below exploit these difficulties.

Are Existing Inequalities Deserved?

You don't have to agree with the frontal assault on desert to recognize that few existing inequalities are deserved. Inequalities of social status are a case in point. To be deserved, these would have to be based on the value judgment that the people at the top are better than those at the bottom. Chapter 3 argued that that judgment just won't wash. The point could easily have been expressed in terms of desert. The following discussion concentrates on another particular area, the income inequalities found in today's capitalist societies, and argues that they too are undeserved.

The work ethic

People sometimes justify their financial success by saying how hard they worked for it. The implication is that hard work is admirable; in fact, that's one of the central tenets of the so-called 'work ethic'. And admirable people ought to be rewarded.

One big problem with this argument is the belief in the work ethic itself. Our society makes people work hard, but is that really such a good thing? Doesn't it at least depend on the kind of work people are doing, and why they're doing it? What's so great, for instance, about working yourself to the bone in the international money market or in the nuclear weapons industry? What's so admirable about working hard if it's only for your own personal gain?

But even if you accept the values of the work ethic, that

won't justify the existing range of incomes. The highest incomes in our society aren't due to hard work at all, but simply to the ownership of wealth. And in the area of 'earned' income, it's obvious to anyone with their eyes open that the people capitalism forces to work the hardest are often the least well paid of all. Thus, present-day incomes just *don't* reward hard work; nor, for the same reason, do they compensate for it.

'Contribution'

A second basis for existing incomes is sometimes put forward under the title 'rewards for contributions'. In academic writing, this has been interpreted as each person deserving to get back from the economy in income what she or he contributes to the economy in production. And economists sometimes say that that's exactly how a free market operates.

Now to make a contribution to society is indeed an admirable thing. But if you take back from the economy everything you're supposed to have 'contributed' to it, what have you contributed then? Answer – nothing at all! And having contributed nothing, you've done nothing admirable. You deserve, in return, absolutely nothing.

Of course, the 'rewards for contributions' argument doesn't have to be put in terms of desert. You might put it like this: 'I made this product; therefore I ought to get it or its equivalent back'. There's nothing especially to do with desert here. You're asserting a property right over what you have made. It's a good question, discussed in Chapter 7, to ask for the basis of such property rights; the point here is that desert is not the answer.

Would people deserve a reward for a real contribution? If, say, half their product went towards building public hospitals, wouldn't they then deserve a reward? Let's say they do: we can call that the social-democratic principle of desert. But what reward is appropriate? Obviously not the other half of their product. If I give a hundred pounds to the Miners' Support Fund, do I deserve a hundred pounds reward for my generosity? Maybe I deserve an expression of thanks, or an honorary doctorate! But financially, surely no more than, say, a pint in the bar: that is, less than one per cent of my gift. It would seem to follow on this revised, social-democratic principle of desert, that something under one per cent of the gross national product should be distributed by desert. Put another way, it means that a person who is a hundred times more productive than average should get just under double the average wage. That's not much to write home about, is it?

In any case contribution arguments depend on the very contentious problem of deciding what a person's 'contribution' is. Defenders of the market constantly mix up the question of how much people contribute to production with the question of how much their contributions can be sold for. You and I might contribute equal effort and skill to a project, but because your skill is in short supply it will fetch a higher price. Who contributes more to people's health, surgeons or sanitation workers? *Obviously* the market is going to reward people's contributions if 'contribution' is defined by what the market rewards! But you don't win an argument by defining your terms to order.

Services rendered

One anti-egalitarian idea which does smack of desert isn't always put in those terms. It comes out, for instance, in a book in which Keith Joseph and Jonathan Sumption first of all criticize rewards for merit as an unworkable *egalitarian* idea, and then go on to defend the market for rewarding people's usefulness (see 'References and Further Reading'). Market prices, they say, show the real value people place on other people's services.

The appeal of this justification surely comes from desert. Why else should the fact that someone's services are *valued* be a good reason for rewarding them? There's a little problem about the low pay of worthy professionals like nurses and teachers, but that doesn't put Joseph and Sumption off their stride. It merely shows that humanity really values their services less than people who have given the world designer jeans.

Unfortunately, the objection won't go away so easily. Markets don't pay for the services people value: they pay for the services people have the money to buy. The resulting income distribution isn't going to have much to do with service to humanity, though it might reflect service to the well-off. And service to the well-off just doesn't count as a human excellence deserving of reward.

Skill

Yet another common argument for deserved income is skill. People assume that skilled workers should be paid more than unskilled workers, that 'professionals' should get more than 'manual workers'. If the argument is just that it takes a certain amount of work to learn a skill and that people deserve to be compensated for this, then it paints a very implausible picture of the hardships of training. How could anyone honestly believe, for instance, that it's harder being a university student than working on a building site?

It's more plausible to interpret the argument in terms of merit desert. People admire skill, and that's what justifies its rewards. But, like the services rendered argument, this ignores the fact that a capitalist economy only rewards the skills people have the money to pay for. In particular, it rewards those skills which the owners and controllers of capital pay for in managers – skills which may have a very different value for the rest of society. More generally, the market rewards *scarce* skills, which isn't the same as more admirable ones. And even where skills are genuinely admirable, there's no need to reward them with income rather than 'token' goods like admiration.

It should be clear by now that desert is a very fertile concept, and its plausible uses can go on and on and on. We haven't exhausted its possibilities, but we've seen some strategies for attacking it. Time and again, the argument has come back to the assumption that some occupations are better than others, and so deserve higher rewards. In other words, inequalities of status are used to justify inequalities of income. One egalitarian reply is to attack the connection between them; the more radical approach is to attack both inequalities at once.

Compensation in an Egalitarian Society

Desert can't be used to defend the way things are. But would it justify inequalities in a good society? The rest of this chapter addresses that question. This section looks at two central issues of compensation – different levels of pay to compensate for different kinds of work, and the 'own-fault' clause which denies you compensation for losses which are your own fault. The next section looks at issues of merit.

Work

The principle of economic equality is at its core a belief that the costs and benefits of socially necessary production should be equally shared. So the simplest way of imagining economic equality is to imagine a society of people who work the same number of hours at tasks which have the same levels of stress, responsibility, effort, risk, and so on, provide the same degree of satisfaction, and furnish them with equal power, prestige, and pay. Modern industrial life makes that society practically impossible to imagine, though maybe it's more of a possibility than it seems. So try to imagine an egalitarian society with a lot of specialized jobs. In that society, some people's duties might involve special costs and difficulties. Since economic life would be a cooperative venture in which everyone felt an obligation to participate, people would deserve to be compensated for those extra burdens. Compensation here would be serving egalitarian aims.

It's doubtful whether everything now talked about as grounds for compensation would cut ice in egalitarian pay negotiations. Responsibility, for instance, is often more satisfying than onerous. So is the exercise of special skills, while the long training they require – a standard part of the rationalizations put forward in our society for the high incomes of 'professionals' – is a pretty flimsy excuse for higher-than-average incomes. Do trainee doctors and lawyers really work harder than if they were in a job or apprenticeship instead? And if they do, shouldn't this be compensated for by giving them better wages and conditions while training than by writing them blank cheques when they qualify?

Dangerous, tiring, stressful, tedious, and dirty jobs are more compelling cases for compensation, a compensation that would tend to reverse rather than reinforce present-day income differentials – starting, perhaps, with better pay for cleaners, cooks, and childminders. Not that this would always mean a higher weekly income: it could mean shorter hours instead. And since there are some things neither time nor money can make up for, compensation arguments should never be expected to replace the need for radical changes in job structures.

What kind of compensating pay differentials, then, might we expect to find in our imagined egalitarian society? That has no reliable answer, but you can make a rough subjective guess by starting with the fact that in 1984 the weekly pay for jobs like carpentry and bricklaying was just about average for British men in full-time manual employment (around £145 per week). Is any job so much harder than these that you would need to be paid more than twice as much for doing them just to balance things off? Personally, I doubt that there is. But on that view, compensating differentials could probably be contained within an income distribution in which the best-paid people earned no more than twice the average. Of course this is only guessing. You can play with different figures if you like, but be honest!

How would compensation levels be set? The distribution of income in our own society depends heavily on market mechanisms, and we've already noted that these react not just to differences in attractiveness but also to the distribution of income and to relative scarcity. But existing incomes are also influenced by custom, management decision, and collective bargaining, in which questions of compensation have always played a part. In an egalitarian society, the extension of democratic planning would allow an even greater role for the deliberate setting of pay scales, in which making a case for a differential could come to depend less on market power and more on proving relative disadvantages. Within such a structure, markets might be used in a way which responded more to the relative attractions of different jobs and less to scarcity. The relationship between markets and planning is really an issue for egalitarian economics, but some of the principles involved are discussed further in Chapter 8.

Choices

'You don't deserve compensation for trouble that's your own fault.' Egalitarians can see some point in that rule. It places an arguably equal burden of responsibility on everyone. It promotes self-reliance, which fosters self-esteem. It recognizes that good will has its limits, that even in an egalitarian society you couldn't expect people to fund extravagant ambitions or to bail you out every time you did something stupid. Finally (though this is really an incentive argument), it encourages people to think about the consequences of their actions. But the rule has big exceptions.

It's easy to hold people responsible for day to day activities – for what they buy, for how they treat their friends and neighbours, for what they do in their spare time. But there are big choices in life which are full of uncertainty, or depend on circumstances, upbringing, emotion, and influence. Choices of education, of job, of spouse, of residence, even of life style – if these choices turn out badly, is it really right to blame the people who make them, and to insist that they bear the consequences? Why not give them a second chance?

The 'own-fault clause' makes sense for day to day affairs, but for such major life decisions the arguments in its favour cease to apply. A policy of unrelieved suffering for past mistakes can't plausibly be described as a way of sharing equally the burdens of choice. And it would be a sick joke to lecture self-reliance to anyone who's trapped in a job or marriage they find oppressive. Good will has its limits, but surely even ordinary good will isn't blind to the point that it's largely a matter of luck whether your life works out well or badly as a whole. And as far as incentives are concerned, bad life decisions are painful enough even when softened by a second chance. Nobody can argue that people have to suffer their full, terrible consequences just to encourage good sense.

There's another point. The argument so far assumes that when we mention 'the full consequences' we know what we're talking about. But of course, in almost any case that matters, the consequences of a person's choice are heavily determined by social arrangements. In our society, the consequences of leaving school at 14 are enormous, but there's nothing inevitable about that. The consequences would be much less severe if there were better access to adult education and greater social equality. And so another way of arguing the case is to agree that people should bear the full consequences of their decisions, but to question just what those consequences should be. Either way, the own-fault clause is limited in scope.

Merit in an Egalitarian Society

Would the broadly equal society envisaged by egalitarians have any room for inequalities based on merit? Would it permit the practice of making value judgments about people and treating them accordingly? I can't imagine this vanishing. But the crucial issues are over the kinds of value judgments made and the kinds of treatment meted out.

It's hard to say much about the content of personal value judgments in an egalitarian society. Egalitarianism has implications for the standards people apply to each other in such central areas of life as sexuality, personality, and work. It's also hard to predict how life in an egalitarian society would affect the inclination to judge others and to set up differences between them. We're so used to people being compared and rewarded or punished that we can't form a very clear picture of a more broad-minded way of life. Any discussion of merit desert in an egalitarian society has to be speculative, and to ask more questions than it answers. It helps to organize the discussion according to whether the value judgment involved is 'private' or 'public'.

Private and public desert

Most day to day judgments about desert depend on 'private' value judgments – that is, on one individual's opinion of another. For instance, you might think that Clint Eastwood is a terrible actor while I rate him as a modern master. So you think he deserves to be scorned, while I think he deserves great praise. Can we really imagine a world without this kind of value judgment and these sorts of views about what people deserve? I doubt it. But is there any good reason to be against them? Would the inequalities they defend – inequalities of popularity, and perhaps of self-esteem – still be open to criticism? There are probably some egalitarians who think so, but it's difficult to see how they could really be avoided.

The case is different when a society starts to institutionalize desert. It then has to go beyond private opinions to value judgments of a more impersonal kind, taken to represent not just one individual's views but the official assessment of some group. We can call this 'public desert'. The tricky thing about public desert is finding an acceptable way of making these public value judgments. In sports, for instance, you sometimes have to develop elaborate contests with complicated rules to make sure that the best players win. In law, jury systems have evolved to judge guilt. Educational institutions have devoted enormous energy to making up fair assessment systems. Even so, everyone knows that these systems are far from perfect.

Sometimes the problem is a disagreement over the standards which should be applied, or even over whether there should be a public judgment at all. Think of the controversy over book prizes, art awards, the Nobel Peace Prize, Miss America. But even when there's a consensus on standards, systems of public value judgment aren't always accurate. Innocent people can be convicted, bad players can win, good students can fail, heroes can go unnoticed.

Public evaluation systems have a natural tendency to end up rewarding your skill at playing the system instead of the skill the system was set up to reward. And because of their publicity, they tend to pick out obvious, visible achievements which might be less admirable than the quiet activities of others. Finally, public systems judge fairly specific abilities, and are blind to a person's other strengths and failings. A businessman may be philanthropic with his wealth, but mean to his employees. An activist may have done a lot for some cause, but be an unreliable friend. All of these problems provide arguments against setting too much store by public value judgments, and are thus arguments against having too substantial a system of public desert. But do they rule out public desert altogether?

What do people publicly deserve?

Given these problems about public evaluation, the easiest deserts to defend are specific, token deserts which do no more then express their underlying value judgments: things like public recognition and criticism, or medals or trophies. Of course, such awards and brickbats can be very important to people, but their importance is precisely the importance attached to the values used to support them. When Daley Thompson won a gold medal in the 1984 Olympics, it wasn't the value of the metal that mattered, but the sense of achieving excellence, of being the best. A token award has as much or as little justification as the specific kind of public evaluation which goes to support it.

By contrast, it seems impossible to defend substantial income differences, differences in personal power, or permanent distinctions of status by merit desert arguments. That would be creating broad differences between people's overall life chances on account of partial comparisons between them. Excellence in singing or accountancy or football deserves recognition for what it is, but it doesn't show that the star of stage, office, or stadium is a better person overall.

The difficult cases for egalitarians are the ones in between. For instance, what about 'token' cash prizes and income differentials? They involve inequality, but if you really think someone deserves recognition, aren't these ways of showing you really mean it? Of putting your money where your mouth is? Another difficult issue is certification. Do people who have learnt certain skills deserve certificates saying so? Our society certainly seems to think so, with our complicated system of academic and trade diplomas and certificates. Certification is supposed to protect consumers against impostors, but it also provides for hierarchies of power and status. It certifies some people as nothing but failures. Wouldn't we be better off without it? Or can it be contained?

Then there's the related question of whether desert should have any role in jobs and education. Since egalitarians believe that *everyone* should have fulfilling education and work, desert couldn't be as important in an egalitarian society as in a meritocracy. But it's hard to imagine that everyone could end up doing just what they'd most like to do. Isn't it an appropriate expression of public admiration of a skill or intellectual achievement to give some people more scope to carry on? Finally, there is the big issue of punishment. Egalitarians have traditionally viewed punishment as a deterrent or as rehabilitation, and have rejected the idea that criminals also deserve to be punished. That view might not be so appealing in a society whose dominant values were themselves egalitarian.

These questions raise issues of principle for egalitarians concerning just how far merit desert can justify inequalities of personal wellbeing. But they do not undermine the arguments for the central equalities which we took in Chapter 1 as a working definition of egalitarianism. They are further questions on the frontier of egalitarian thinking.

Desert and human worth

There is one merit desert argument which is thoroughly egalitarian. It is the argument that because it's a valuable thing just to be human, all human beings deserve respect as persons and concern for their wellbeing. This is a perfectly proper desert argument based on a value judgment about being human, and if you listen to egalitarian political arguments you'll often hear some version of it. Of course, if you want to rely on it, you have to believe in the equal fundamental worth of all human beings. I don't know any way of arguing for that, but there don't seem to be any arguments against it either. It's the sort of belief you might expect to find in a society free from the pervasive social prejudices we've all imbibed as children. And it's a convenient way to make desert work for equality, not against it.

Two Impossible Dreams

The arguments of this chapter relate to the world as it is or might be. Here are two objections which aren't so realistic.

Suppose everyone started with equal money. Then surely any inequalities people earned from market transactions would indicate the value of their services to others, and so would be deserved.

This argument is a response to the point that in an unequal society, the market rewards not valuable services but only services people can pay for. Well, let's assume an equal division of wealth and a market, and let's assume for the sake of argument that the market produces inequalities which we treat as deserved rewards for people's services. What then? Do we keep the market going? But that would be a market in an unequal society, and its results would veer away from desert. Or do we freeze things after, so to speak, one 'round' of trading? That doesn't give the market very much of a role! The argument is self-defeating, because it tries to justify inequalities by a strategy which presupposes equality.

Maybe people who are excellent in only one way don't deserve a better life than others. But if you're a better person overall, surely you do deserve a better life.

The argument earlier on was that partial comparisons between people were obviously inadequate justifications for general differences between them. It doesn't follow that overall comparisons *would* be sufficient grounds for such differences.

Why wouldn't they just be grounds for public recognition and other token rewards?

In any case, what would count as being 'a better person overall'? Would you have to be better at everything? Or would it be enough to be morally better? After all, a 'good person' usually means a morally good one. Are we to have public tribunals for ranking people overall, and institutions for ensuring that the good prosper and the wicked perish?

Of course, you are perfectly free to carry around your own standards of personal excellence, and to think of some people as altogether more worthy than others. And you would be perfectly free, even in an egalitarian society, to rail against the injustice of good people being miserable and bad people being happy – even, within the overall framework set by egalitarianism, to do what you could to put things right. But there would doubtless be others who disagreed, and still others who, while agreeing with your standards, nevertheless considered it absurd and ridiculous to set up public systems of overall evaluation.

7

Would Equality
Restrict Freedom?

In contemporary politics, anti-egalitarians have tried to corner
the market on freedom. They say they stand for 'free
enterprise', for 'freedom to choose', for the defence of the
'free world'. But egalitarians have also claimed to stand for
freedom, as the classic slogan 'liberty, equality, fraternity'
proclaims. Which side is right? Is equality really incompatible
with freedom?

'Equality versus Freedom' is a handy slogan, but it's
simplistic. Equality is a complicated idea and freedom is too.
Just as there are many equalities, there are many freedoms –
from freedom of speech to freedom from hunger, from the
'free market' to women's liberation. But just as political
debate tends to concentrate on particular kinds of equality, so
it concentrates on particular kinds of freedom. The freedoms
most commonly brought up are the freedom to develop and
use your talents, the 'economic freedom' of owning, buying,
and selling, and the 'political freedoms' of speech, assembly,
and democratic participation.

The Standard Egalitarian Position

Egalitarians have taken up this issue time and again, and have
developed two general strategies for dealing with it. The first
strategy is to expose a bias in the anti-egalitarian case. It pays
a lot of attention to certain kinds of *state* power, but it

completely ignores *economic* power. Businesses exercise tremendous power over the individual as employers, bankers, manufacturers, and retailers, and can restrict freedom just as effectively as the state does. So if you're really interested in freedom, you should be interested in limiting and controlling not just political power but economic power, too.

The second strategy used by egalitarians is to argue that a person's freedom is just as much limited by a lack of resources as by external barriers. Is a poor person free to go to the theatre? Legally free, yes, but prevented by poverty from doing so. Aren't class barriers just as intimidating as force when it comes to getting an education or dealing with the legal system? And doesn't ignorance obstruct free choice as effectively as any bureaucracy? But then the satisfaction of basic needs, and equalities of income, power, and status, wouldn't *restrict* freedom, they would merely extend to everyone the freedoms currently enjoyed by the privileged.

Anti-egalitarians typically rebut these arguments by saying that neither is really about freedom. To the charge of economic power, they reply that no one in a market economy is really forced to do anything, since people choose their jobs and their purchases. Their reply to the second strategy is that, by definition, freedom can only be restricted by force or coercion, not by lack of resources.

One weakness of this rebuttal is that the market economy itself and the privileges it creates are upheld by the coercive power of the law. Consumers may be free to purchase what they like, but they're certainly not free to take what they like without paying for it! In any case, it's obvious that people's choices are severely restricted by economic structures and by a lack of power, money, position, and knowledge. These are real restrictions on their lives, affect them just as strongly as open coercion, are just as much the results of human action, and are in principle just as open to alteration. In terms of what matters in life, they are so similar to cases of coercion that, whether you call them a matter of freedom or not, they are equally important.

Anti-egalitarians are on stronger ground when they argue that any freedoms achieved through greater equality would involve the loss of other, more important freedoms. In particular, they argue that an egalitarian society would have to restrict the freedom of individuals to develop their capacities and exploit their talents; it would have to curb people's freedom to use their rightful property; and it would inevitably involve the removal of cherished political freedoms such as free speech and the right to organize politically. Is that true?

The Freedom to Develop your Talents

Critics claim that egalitarianism would stifle individual self-development and prevent people from employing their talents to the full. For how could an equal society permit anyone to become an exceptional musician or painter or athlete or lawyer? This is a simple misunderstanding which confuses the idea of equality with the idea of everyone being the same. Egalitarianism has nothing against excellence. It's strongly committed to giving everyone the means to develop their particular capacities in a satisfying and fulfilling way. By contrast, our present social structures only allow this to a privileged few.

Perhaps what the objectors have in mind is the idea that an egalitarian society would force people to develop certain *kinds* of talents. They project an image of equality as a huge bureaucratic machine which assesses everyone and directs them into appropriate positions. The people best suited to be teachers would have to become teachers, even if they wanted to try something else. But that's no less of a misunderstanding, since forcing people into careers they dislike would also be incompatible with the commitment to satisfying and fulfilling self-development. Of course, *every* social structure places *some* limits on choices of training and career. In our own society, these limits are for most of the population severely narrow. An egalitarian society could not, perhaps, guarantee to everyone the best conceivable opportunities for developing their capacities. But it could use strategies like job restructuring and continuing education to give people a lot more freedom than they have now.

It's hard to escape the conclusion, though, that these complaints about egalitarianism are really standing in for something else. For when you look in newspapers and magazines for supposed examples of individual freedom, what you find are endless descriptions of people who start from nothing and become rich: unemployed youths who become pop stars, mail boys who become company directors, and so on. The real issue here is not whether equality would prevent people from developing their capacities, but whether it would stop them from selling those capacities to the highest bidder. An egalitarian society wouldn't prevent people from becoming pop stars, but it would limit their incomes. People would be free to develop their skills in medicine, law, finance, or management, but they wouldn't be able to use these skills to make a fortune.

Not that people wouldn't benefit at *all* from developing and using their capacities. After all, they would share in the total output of the society, and it's only through the use of their abilities that there would be any output to begin with. What egalitarian principles regulate is the form of this interaction. Instead of a system where people's rewards are determined by the price their abilities can fetch on the market and the power they have over economic resources, an egalitarian system would be geared to people's real needs, and to compensating them for the real difficulties of their work. It would change the degree to which people benefited from using their capacities, with some people benefiting more than they do now, and others less. But there isn't anything particularly *unfree* about that.

The Freedoms of Ownership

It's common knowledge that equality conflicts with private property. That's what connects egalitarianism to socialism. But anti-egalitarians argue that an attack on property is a double attack on freedom. First, and obviously, it attacks the freedom to use one's property. Secondly, it attacks the personal freedoms property protects. And they place these arguments within a long tradition of political philosophy. These arguments are so commonsensical and seem so obvious that it takes a little unravelling to show what's wrong with them. But they're bad arguments nonetheless.

What is property?

What is it to own something – say, this book? It's not as simple as, for instance, having it in your pocket. That's only a matter of its location. Ownership is a matter of rights – and not even of a single right, but of complicated *sets* of rights. If you own this book, you have the right to keep it, to read it without interference, to give it away, to throw it in the bin, to use it to prop up a table, to sell it or swap it or rent it. *Your* owning the book gives *you* these rights, and at the same time denies them to everyone else. No one else is allowed to handle, read, or dispose of your book without your permission.

What does this reveal about freedom and property? Well, your ownership of a piece of property enhances *your* freedom, since it leaves you free to use that property in many ways. But it restricts *everyone else's* freedom to do precisely the same things. If everyone had roughly the same amount of property, they'd have roughly similar freedom of this kind; but if property is very unequally distributed, then some people have a lot of freedom and others very little. There is no general connection between the mere existence of property and extensive personal freedom – it all depends, at least, on how property is distributed.

Property systems

Ownership does not, however, leave you completely free to do what you like with your property. As things stand, you are not free to throw this book at a policeman, to photocopy more than ten per cent of it, to sell it under a different cover, or to plagiarize it. Though the rules vary from case to case, ownership is never the complete freedom to do what you want with an object. That would involve too much loss of freedom on the part of others.

In general, for anything you can think of, you can imagine many different systems of rights and restrictions connecting that thing to people. Each of these systems would be a system of property. Imagine car ownership involving the right to drive as fast as you like, or land ownership involving the right to build whatever you fancy. Imagine that owning cigarettes did not involve the right to smoke them in public places, or that owning money did not involve the right to take it out of the country. Imagine that bookshops were more like libraries, and people were expected to bring books back when they were finished with them. All these systems of property are similar to our present systems in some ways and different in others. It is a perfectly valid question to ask which systems of property offer the greatest personal freedom overall.

In view of the fact that property rights always restrict the freedom of non-owners, and that any system of property rights is a combination of various rights and restrictions, it would be simplistic to believe that egalitarians are anti-property and therefore anti-freedom. Instead, you have to ask which property rights egalitarians can support and which they must oppose, and whether the property systems so defined are really more hostile to freedom than the systems we know.

Personal property versus capital

For instance, there are no obvious egalitarian objections to owning a wide range of items for personal use and consumption: food, clothing, furniture, TVs, tennis balls, tools, even books! So long as this kind of ownership were widely dispersed, there would seem to be more freedom involved in keeping it than in changing it. Egalitarians must surely agree, too, that a monetary system and the use of consumer markets is for the most part a harmless way of organizing the distribution of these goods. There are no serious egalitarian grounds for stopping people giving such goods as presents, or swapping them, or using them to build bookshelves or to grow vegetables. Egalitarians need have no qualms about the right to occupy a house or apartment, to decorate it and furnish it as you like, to receive visitors into it as and when you like. These are property rights which everyone can have, protecting freedoms which everyone can enjoy, and there is no reason to expect them to generate or perpetuate major inequalities.

The only property rights egalitarians have to object to are the ones which prop up existing inequalities or would undermine any egalitarian alternative. In our own society, the main rights concerned are those of the owners and controllers of capital – rights which allow them to buy and control other people's labour. In an egalitarian society, property rights would be designed to prevent any return of inequality: for instance, by restricting the growth and character of private employment, or by placing a ceiling on personal incomes. Like other societies, it would provide a legal framework within which people could make reasonably clear and reliable plans. This would consist of general rules, not day to day bureaucratic controls over people's choices. But it would be structured to produce egalitarian effects when people followed those rules, and in particular to prevent the re-emergence of capitalism. The design of such a system is, of course, a difficult problem of socialist economics, involving questions concerning appropriate forms of planning and of markets. But there's no reason to consider it impossible.

Capital and freedom

These egalitarian revisions of people's property rights would leave some people unable to do some of the things they can now do, such as direct the use of capital, and so would restrict their freedom. But to discover the overall impact this has on freedom, we have to look at the other freedoms and unfreedoms which those property rights perpetuate. The most obvious point is that the freedom of a privileged minority to control the means of production corresponds to a lack of such freedom on the part of everyone else. You can get an indication of how small a minority we're talking about from the fact that in Britain, three quarters of all privately owned company shares belong to 2.5 per cent of the population; in the US, the proportion is even smaller, perhaps as little as one per cent. In both countries, economic activity is dominated by large companies, whose directors, top executives, and principal shareholders account for less than a thousandth of the population.

Property rights over capital are primarily rights over the means of production, but they also generate inequalities of wealth and power. And wealth and power have, in turn, an important impact on other freedoms. Obviously the wealthy enjoy an extensive freedom of choice as consumers, and many of the goods and services they can buy are themselves freedom-enhancing: labour-saving consumer durables, travel, houses with more security and privacy, country retreats. Their domestic servants – cleaners, nannies, and gardeners – free them from household chores. They have considerable freedom over their choice of career (for the very rich, over whether to work at all); and this freedom is passed on from one generation to the next through private schooling, family and business connections, and inherited wealth. Once established in their well-heeled jobs, they have a wide range of choice over how they spend their time, organizing their own timetables, sorting out for themselves how to tackle the work in hand, and delegating the tedious stuff to underlings. All this freedom is expanded, in general, by a lack of close supervision. At the end of the year, of course, results of various kinds have to be achieved or 'heads will roll'. But there's no one breathing down their necks in the meantime.

The contrast with typical members of the worst-off groups in society is obvious. A low income not only restricts your choice of purchases, but precludes purchasing just those goods and services which could positively extend your freedom. You have a narrow choice of 'careers' (even the word is denied you). If you've got a job, it is probably tightly controlled in terms of hours, duties, and chain of command. You are as unfree during working hours as any slave, and your employer can often exercise considerable control over your outside activities, too. If you've become a housewife, your tasks are highly specific, often monotonous, and subject to often conflicting yet uncompromising demands from your family. You are dependent on your husband and physically isolated. *You* are doing the kind of domestic chores which rich people pay others to do for them. If you are unemployed, you are subjected to the regimentation and humiliation of the dole queue. Even your 'free' time isn't your own, since how you spend it can affect your entitlements. Finally, if you try to start up a business, either personally or cooperatively, you face huge obstacles. It is almost impossible to get adequate finance if you don't own property already. You chain yourself and your family to long hours and backbreaking work. And in the end, it's still a risky business: in Britain, for instance, about half of all small businesses fail within six years.

Now, the question we have set ourselves is whether the freedom enjoyed by the owners and controllers of capital can be justified in terms of freedom itself. How could anyone honestly say so, when it is responsible for such a gross lack of freedom on the part of others? How could anyone think that the freedom of a tiny minority to control the means of production is more important than the freedom of far greater numbers of people to choose interesting and worthwhile careers, to have control over their working lives, to have enough money to exercise real choice over what they buy? Capitalist property rights are not an issue of freedom versus equality, but of freedom for a few versus freedom for everyone. For anybody who really cares about freedom, the choice must be obvious.

Property and Freedom in a Socialist Economy

The criticism of capitalism as an unfree social system does not imply that a good society would have no property rights, but only different ones. A good society's property relations would operate so as to ensure that important freedoms are enjoyed by everyone: freedoms over life styles, jobs, decision making, and so on. It is reasonable to call these relations socialist, since they extend key freedoms and other benefits throughout society, and have the effect of placing the economy under social as opposed to private control.

But socialism is often taken to mean much less – to mean no more than an economic system in which the major means of production are state-owned. And so an economy can be socialist even if it's run by a bureaucratic elite whose privileges are scarcely distinguishable from those of capitalists; whose freedom to control resources is matched by a lack of control by everyone else; who enjoy an extensive freedom of choice in consumption which is denied to others; who are the only people free to choose interesting and self-directing careers. In such an economy, the key property rights which sustain capitalist inequality are paralleled by the rights which this elite exercises over productive resources and which they can use to sustain their other privileges, even if some property rights (such as sale and bequest) are largely absent.

The key task of an egalitarian socialist society – or as you might prefer to call it, a truly socialist society – would be to structure the control of resources in aid of *everyone's* freedom. There is little point in simply replacing one privileged class by another. In broad terms, the problem is how to control resources democratically – how to establish an equality of power over the way resources are used, through a combination of collective decisions and individual rights. Socialism and democracy are inseparable.

There is a tradition in politics which asserts that property is connected with freedom: we can now see the sense in which that tradition is correct. For freedom is extended to everyone only in a socialist society. And a society is truly socialist only if control over productive resources is exercised democratically. But control over productive resources is, of course, a kind of property right. So freedom does depend on property, only not in an old-fashioned way.

Political Freedom

Many people think that egalitarianism poses a threat not just to economic freedom but to political freedom as well. The source of this belief isn't hard to find – it's that equality is associated with socialism, which is associated in turn with repressive political systems. But associations don't make an argument. Would equality really bring tyranny in its wake?

The simplest explanation of a connection between equality and authoritarianism is the idea that equality could only be brought about by a centralized state which had total control of the economy. Such a state would necessarily be in the hands of a bureaucratic elite who would use their absolute power to stifle all opposition: stripping dissenters of their livelihood, preventing access to the mass media, and prohibiting the distribution of political pamphlets. After all, isn't that what *has* happened in the USSR and elsewhere?

The answer to this argument should be obvious from the last section. It is that any socialist economy run by a bureaucratic elite will lack even economic equality, never mind political. That kind of 'socialism' is as objectionable to egalitarians as to anyone else. Economic equality doesn't threaten democratic rights; on the contrary, it depends on them. So the argument makes a valid criticism of bureaucracy, but falsely associates it with equality.

Shall we try a more sophisticated argument? It is that however decisions are formally organized, governments can only be held in check if citizens are equipped to organize, state opposing views, publicize their case. That needs money. 'How much money is required,' remarks J.R. Lucas, 'depends on the enterprise. Any civic society or amenity group is far more effective if one of its supporters is a businessman who can get things typed by his secretary or copied on the firm's xerox.' The general conclusion is that rich and/or influential people are necessary to keep the 'bureaucratic juggernaut' at bay.

Ask yourself what sorts of political cause Lucas's business-man is likely to support. The argument is once again not a defence of freedom, but of the freedom of the privileged. No matter how many wealthy supporters can be mustered by the poor and powerless, their opponents can match their resources many times over. What sort of freedom is that?

The democratic structures of an egalitarian society would *of course* have to include all kinds of provisions for the protection of minorities, for the expression of opinions, for restraining bureaucrats. Decisions both in traditionally political matters and in the economy would be more accountable than now, more open to criticism and debate. But that process would be accessible to everyone, not just to the pals of businessmen!

To all this, a third argument replies that such an open democratic system could not possibly work in favour of equality. Its formally equal access would in fact enable some groups – those with special skills, unusual cohesion, more political cop-on – to advance their own, sectional interests and to establish unequal positions for themselves. 'The most effective way of holding such groups in check,' wrote Frank Parkin in a much-quoted passage, 'is by denying them the right to organize politically.' In short, an egalitarian state would have to restrict the freedom of its opponents.

The argument assumes that the free political activity of clever reactionaries would threaten an egalitarian system. But how? By opening the possibility of majority support for inequality? Well, any democratic government runs the risk of being voted out of office. An egalitarian government would by its own principles have to resign if a majority turned against it. Suppose, on the other hand, that an anti-egalitarian minority were organizing the forcible overthrow of a popularly elected, democratic socialist government. You would not be violating but defending political freedom if you took steps against that.

Maybe the argument is that since an open, 'pluralist' democracy responds to and makes compromises between pressure groups, the activities of anti-egalitarians would somehow *have* to produce inequalities. But this entirely depends on the nature and strength of the commitments of the rest of society. In pluralist political systems, groups influence the kinds of decision which it is generally agreed they have a right to influence. It's forbidden for them to operate in other areas (appointments which are supposed to be on merit, legal judgments which are supposed to be objective, and so on). That isn't considered a denial of political freedom. Once egalitarian practices became part of the framework of social relations, their opponents could only challenge them by transforming a whole social ethos, not by political manoeuvring.

This reply suggests a fourth argument. It's that even if political freedom would be secure in a fully egalitarian society, it would have to be restricted to get there. How else could socialists possibly overcome the power of capitalism? Well, many socialists do believe that any serious challenge to capitalism must ultimately be by force of arms and involve the suspension of political rights. The onus is on them to show how these methods can avoid a permanent dictatorship not so much 'of' as 'in the name of' ordinary working people. If a majority of the population cannot be convinced of socialist ideas in the face of right-wing propaganda, how likely is it that they will be convinced once they have suffered the confusion, bloodshed, and repression of a violent revolution?

It is much more plausible to suppose that only a popularly elected majority government, recognized as legitimate even by its opponents, could achieve the extension of democracy which true socialism requires. Of course it would use political power to carry out its aims, and like any government would have to protect itself. The history of left-wing governments is crowded with attempted coups and foreign-backed invasions, and such governments have often faced hard choices about political freedoms in times of national emergency. No one can pretend that future socialist governments wouldn't have the same problems. But these problems are ultimately concerned with defending freedom, not abandoning it.

Meanwhile, let no one forget the power exercised by privileged minorities in our own society: their influence on government policies, their ability to shape public opinion, their organizational and financial advantages as pressure groups and lobbyists. Anyone who thinks that we already live in a paradise of political freedom which equality could only destroy should think again. The truth is exactly the opposite – that only a thoroughly egalitarian society could secure the political liberties most of us claim to believe in.

Equality as Freedom

All these arguments help to explain why the principles of equality are often considered principles of human liberation. The satisfaction of needs means freedom from the narrow constraints of personal hardship; it means the basic standard of living on which all other freedoms depend. The principle of equal respect means freedom from degradation, exploitation, and the oppression of social rank. Economic equality means having the freedoms that come with a decent income; it means freeing employees from the tyranny of bosses; it means freedom to develop your capacities in a satisfying way; it means freeing politics from the domination of the rich. Political equality means extending democratic freedoms to all of society. Sexual, racial, ethnic, and religious equality mean freedom from major forms of social and economic oppression.

People who reject equality are rejecting freedom, too.

Schools, Markets, and Bequests

This chapter has concentrated on the broad issue of equality and freedom. Here are some objections based mostly on some particular applications.

Egalitarianism would surely prevent some skills from flourishing – for instance entrepreneurial talent. So it doesn't really leave people free to develop their capacities.

In fact, a socialist economy needs a lot of what goes into 'entrepreneurial flair': spotting new ways to produce things, conceiving new forms of organization, anticipating changes of taste, arranging financial backing, managing a workplace. Perhaps a socialist 'entrepreneur' has to convince a democratically structured 'bank' to invest funds, and has to lead rather than direct a labour force, but the skills involved are not so different. The main difference is that this entrepreneur wouldn't end up with five hundred times the income of a fellow worker. That's a difference in how much you benefit from the use of your capacities, not in whether you can use them.

Of course, some talents would be redundant: for certain kinds of wheeling and dealing, for making it big in the money market. But every society discourages and suppresses some talents and encourages others. Capitalism encourages the talents for which there is greatest economic demand, which is not the same as those most urgently needed; it limits the development of talents which poor people need but cannot pay for, such as house-building and teaching skills; it discourages in nearly everyone the use of certain capacities – for cooperation, democratic participation, critical analysis; it denies to many people both the education and the employment necessary for developing any satisfying talents at all. And nobody needs to teach capitalism anything about the idea of a redundant skill! Maybe a socialist society couldn't allow every human potential to thrive, but it could hardly be more restrictive than what we've got.

What about education? Wouldn't egalitarian schools restrict gifted children? And wouldn't parents be denied the freedom to send their children to private schools where they'd be more challenged?

Egalitarian education is not aimed at making everyone the same, or at bringing everyone to the same levels of ability, but at encouraging each person to develop her or his capacities in a satisfying and fulfilling way. So it is committed in principle to treating people with different capacities differently. How this works out in practice is of course open to much pedagogical debate, but the debate isn't about *whether* to bring out the best in the brightest students, it's about *how* to bring out the best. Egalitarians simply reject the idea that you can't develop everyone's capacities: that you have to choose between 'bright' and 'slow' children. But it's worth noticing that if education did have to choose, then every system would be restrictive, not just egalitarian ones.

It does not necessarily follow that egalitarians would eliminate parental choice of schools, or even some opportunities to buy education. In our society, where parental 'choice' and private education reinforce gross inequalities, there are good egalitarian arguments against them, and those arguments would presumably apply to some kinds of choice in a different society. But it's not inconceivable that schools might vary in different ways, say by offering different subjects, or different sports, or employing different methods of teaching. In an egalitarian society, those differences might be reasons for providing a choice that wouldn't undermine equality. Nor does there seem to be anything very objectionable about having some provision for buying additional education, particularly for adults. There's no inequality between someone who has to pay for evening classes and someone who has to pay to go to the movies, if these represent their different ways of enjoying themselves and expanding their horizons.

It may not be unfree to prevent people from gaining from the use of their capacities, but it's unfair. After all, their capacities are their own capacities. Don't they have a right to use their own capacities as they wish?

This objection takes possession of capacities to be a kind of property right, and assumes that this property right *contains* the right to sell the use of your capacities on a 'free' market. But this is just what's under dispute. Why should your relation to your capacities involve just *those* property rights, instead of the ones you'd have in an egalitarian society?

Surely there's a difference between the unequal form of capitalism we have now and capitalism as such. Wouldn't a policy of wider home and share ownership be just as egalitarian as socialism?

Egalitarians have nothing in principle against home ownership if it's part of a general policy of decent housing for all. What's objectionable is a policy which promotes ownership but ignores the needs of tenants and the homeless.

As for share ownership, egalitarians have always supported workers' cooperatives – businesses which are genuinely owned and controlled by their employees. By contrast, the currently fashionable idea of a 'share-owning democracy' does nothing to change basic inequalities of wealth and power. It doesn't change the distribution of wealth, but only how personal savings are held; and it doesn't give ordinary shareholders any real control over management. All it does is to disguise inequality by tying more people into the system.

It's one thing to restrict people from accumulating and using capital, but quite another to stop peasants from selling their own produce or small merchants from marketing clothes or thermos bottles. Yet egalitarians must surely suppress those activities, too – as indeed they have done to some extent in every socialist country. Isn't that a restriction of freedom?

The relation between markets and freedom is simply another way of describing the relation between property and freedom, since markets are places where people use the property rights of buying and selling. As we've seen, property rights enhance the freedom of the people who have them and restrict the freedom of everyone else. Thus the simple equation of markets with freedom is untrue. Small-time transactions in a local marketplace between people with equally strong property rights don't necessarily upset equality at all, and might well be compatible with freedom. But markets aren't always so harmless.

In a capitalist economy, workers enter the labour market with only one commodity: their ability to work. They are free to sell this or to suffer. Practically everything else in the world – everything they need for a decent life, everything they need even to produce goods for sale – is owned by others, protected by force of law. How could anyone who cares about freedom approve of that?

An egalitarian society needn't ban all markets, but it has to structure its economy so that everyone's freedom is protected. That means developing property systems which won't give some people tremendous freedom at everyone else's expense.

What about inheritance? Would people in an egalitarian society be free to pass personal property on to their children? Or is this another kind of freedom egalitarianism restricts?

The issue of inherited wealth is closely related to questions of equal opportunity and desert. When people compete for privileges in an unequal society, it seems unfair for some to have the head start of an inherited fortune. And certainly they can't be said to deserve their wealth. So inheritance upsets the objectives of an equal-opportunity meritocracy: nineteenth-century liberalism produced both death duties and the civil service exam.

In an egalitarian society, inheritance would not be such a serious issue. Since no one would have very much more wealth than anyone else, people's inheritances wouldn't differ by much either. And personal wealth in an egalitarian society wouldn't function as capital. Inheritance would not be the transfer of social power that it is now.

An egalitarian policy on inheritance would be aimed at ensuring the long-term stability of equality, and so could only be worked out as part of a whole structure of property rights. It might, for instance, involve an upper limit on the amount anyone could inherit, but it might also turn out that no such restriction was needed because large personal fortunes simply couldn't be accumulated. In either case, the point would be to protect everyone's freedom by preventing the reemergence of capitalist economic relations.

Theorizing that property rights might be different is all very well, but it doesn't change the fact that in our society people already have certain property rights. Surely it would be wrong to violate those rights, even in the name of greater freedom.

One answer to this objection is to draw a distinction between having a legal right and having a moral right. Egalitarianism would of course change people's legal property rights. But on this view nobody's moral rights would be violated because those legal rights were never morally legitimate to begin with. This answer stresses the importance of looking behind the legal and social institutions which create rights to ask whether those institutions are themselves justifiable.

A different answer is to agree that people do now have certain rights, precisely because of existing legal and social institutions. So anyone who simply takes or damages your property really is violating your rights. But since property rights are nothing more than the product of legal and social institutions, changing these institutions can't itself violate any rights; it simply alters them.

The choice of answer depends on theoretical issues about the nature of property rights. But note that neither answer denies that rights exist, or that there may be good reasons for a system of rights. What the two answers have in common is the demand that the rights be justified.

If everything were equally divided tomorrow, all our inequalities would reappear by the end of the week.

This objection, which is at least two hundred years old and is probably expressed two hundred times a day, involves a simple mistake. It assumes that egalitarians would simply redistribute property without changing the rules of ownership – the systems of property. As we have seen, that assumption is false.

Even in its own terms, the objection is implausible. It underestimates the difficulty of accumulating wealth by consent. Anyone who thinks that that's how capitalism got going in the first place should read Marx's description in *Capital*. Capitalism came into the world 'dripping from head to toe, from every pore, with blood and dirt'.

8

Does Society Benefit
from Inequality?

'A little equality's all right but you can have too much of it. It
drags everyone down. It destroys initiative, self-reliance,
drive. It creates an atmosphere of grey uniformity. It's the
mark of a society in decline.' So they say. Americans like to
say it about Britain, and the British like to say it about
themselves. 'What's the point of giving everyone equal shares
of an ever-diminishing cake? Better for society as a whole to
have the inequalities necessary to produce the cake in the first
place!'

Are these claims true? Or is there more truth in the equally
common belief that more equality creates a stronger sense of
community, more teamwork, greater personal commitment?
Time and again, the issue comes back to the question of
motivation, with anti-egalitarians arguing that only inequality
provides the incentive for people to work harder and produce
more. This chapter refutes that argument. It also takes up the
claim that egalitarianism would extend the 'dead hand of
bureaucracy' over every area of life. Finally, it considers one
of the standard arguments against 'too much democracy'. It's
an argument you don't hear quite so often these days,
doubtless because demands for more democracy are in
temporary retreat. But it's by no means disappeared. All of
these arguments are based on the notion of benefit to society
as a whole, so it's worth starting off by having a critical look at
what that really means.

Who Really Benefits When 'Society' Benefits?

Everyday political argument is crowded with claims about the public interest and benefits to society, about the welfare of the community and the general good, about efficiency and waste, growth and recession. Although these claims vary in focus and nuance, they all involve looking at the effects of policies on 'society as a whole', rather than, for instance, at whether a policy violates some individual's rights, or satisfies someone's needs, or gives each person what she or he deserves.

Such a varied and frequently employed set of concepts can mean almost anything – or nothing! But more often than not, principles expressed in terms of the good of the whole have egalitarian overtones. For instance, one of the declared aims of the United States Constitution is to 'promote the general welfare'. The natural way to understand this is that the constitution is meant to benefit every American, with special emphasis, perhaps, on those most in need. The statement is just *false* if it turns out that the constitution only helps New York businessmen while it lets the poor go to the wall. The constitution is supposed to make life better for people in general, not just for a particular section of society.

A policy which benefits people in general doesn't necessarily benefit everyone equally. For instance, a decision to ban smoking in buses may be in the public interest and yet be particularly good for non-smokers and bus cleaners. But over time, we expect decisions based on the public interest to balance out in their effects, without making some people a lot better off than average and others a lot worse. In their everyday political use, terms like 'benefit to society' and 'the public interest' are expected to operate in broadly egalitarian ways.

Utilitarianism

It's natural to suppose that social benefit is a much simpler idea. For you might think that it requires no more than seeing whether the costs of a policy to some people are outweighed by the benefits to others. On that view, a policy benefits society if it produces a *net* benefit after adding up all the costs and benefits to different people. More generally, one policy is better than another if it produces a greater net benefit or a lower net cost.

The position that social benefit in this sense should be the ultimate standard for judging every social issue is called 'utilitarianism'; and it's clear that this utilitarian standard is in principle perfectly compatible with inequality. If it turned out over time that utilitarian decisions produced substantial inequalities of condition, utilitarians would merely conclude that these inequalities were justified.

In practice, many utilitarians do believe in equality. They argue that it's obviously beneficial to satisfy people's basic needs; more generally, they argue that a given amount of income – say £10 a week – means more to a poor person than to a rich one. So if you transfer income from the rich to the poor, there's going to be a net benefit. In politics, utilitarians have usually supported democracy, on the grounds that democratic decisions are more likely to reflect the overall balance of costs and benefits. They've criticized racism, sexism, and religious intolerance because of the deep harm these cause to both their victims and their perpetrators. And utilitarians recognize the great social benefits to be gained by developing a sense of community and mutual respect.

Be that as it may, there are undoubtedly utilitarians who believe that society sometimes benefits from inequalities. And even if they were all egalitarians, that wouldn't make up for the fact that their basic conception of social benefit is open to serious criticisms. One way of summarizing many of these criticisms is that utilitarianism shifts the focus of moral and political thinking away from individual people by completely detaching 'costs' and 'benefits' from the people who experience them. This shift shows up in a number of ways: in a lack of concern for how costs and benefits are distributed, in an inability to account for the priority of basic needs and human rights, in a blindness to the special duties and privileges of personal friendship, in a neglect of questions about personal integrity. The utilitarian view is thus too simplistic for the complexities of social and political life. Maybe that's why, in the real political world, the utilitarian conception of social benefit isn't the most important threat to equality. Instead, the major challenge to equality comes from a related idea called 'benefit-all'.

Benefit-all arguments

Imagine that you lived in an egalitarian society, but one with a pretty low standard of living. And suppose that a certain group of people had special skills which they could use to make life better for everyone, for instance by inventing new products or organizing things more efficiently. But let's imagine that they wouldn't cooperate unless everyone agreed to pay them a higher income than anyone else. Since everyone would benefit from that deal, wouldn't it be worth making?

Arguments for agreeing to deals like this are called 'benefit-all arguments'. In general, they argue for inequalities which make *everyone* better off than they'd be in a situation of equality. Their power comes from the fact that they appeal to the very values that egalitarians themselves say they believe in. For if you care about people's needs and wellbeing, how could you possibly turn down the chance of everyone being better off, even at the cost of some inequalities?

Strong as benefit-all arguments seem, they are not invincible. For benefit-all arguments have certain general features which leave openings for criticism. First of all, benefit-all arguments always contrast an 'equal' situation with an 'unequal' one. It's not unusual for the comparisons to involve a mistaken idea of what egalitarians really believe, for instance in maintaining that equality means everyone having exactly the same income. Secondly, benefit-all arguments always maintain that everyone is better off in the unequal situation than in the equal one. But often their idea of what counts as 'better off' – their idea of personal wellbeing – is open to criticism. Thirdly, benefit-all arguments operate by asserting chains of cause and effect, which state that the social and psychological effects of equality or inequality lead in turn to certain effects on people's wellbeing. For instance, they often claim that only material gain can motivate people to do work which will benefit others. These assertions of fact aren't always true. Finally, of course, benefit-all arguments are like any argument prone to mistakes in reasoning.

The discussion below shows how these four features can be used to defeat benefit-all arguments. In each, the anti-egalitarian case looks more plausible than it really is because of mistaken ideas of equality and of wellbeing, dubious statements of fact, and bad reasoning. These are the major targets to look for in constructing responses to benefit-all arguments.

The Incentive Myth

The most common benefit-all argument is an economic argument based on incentives. It goes like this. Obviously, everyone will be better off if people work hard, if they do the jobs they're best at, and if the best people do the most important jobs. But people won't do these things without an incentive. If everyone gets paid the same no matter what they do, then nobody's got any incentive to do what's useful to society as a whole. It's only by paying people different wages for different jobs that you can get them to work where they're most needed, and it's only by paying them by results that you can get them to work for as long and as hard as they ought to. In short, inequalities act as incentives which benefit everyone. Is this incentive argument sound?

The double standard

Consider the following two arguments.

Jimmy would only get £10 a week more as a building labourer than he gets on the dole.	Mr Brown would only get £5000 a year more as managing director than he gets as a production manager.
So Jimmy has no incentive to work.	So Mr Brown has no incentive to work for a promotion.
So unemployed people should get lower dole.	So managing directors should get higher salaries.

Both arguments are perfectly familiar, yet put side by side it's easy to see the double standard involved. The conclusions could just as well be that building labourers should be paid more and production managers less.

Pointing out the double standard doesn't show that no one needs incentives, but it does show how easy it is for a perfectly simple idea to get turned into a weapon for the rich to use against the poor. Yet even if everyday incentive arguments are fishy, isn't the basic point of the incentive argument right?

How big do incentives have to be?

Let's accept for the sake of argument that pay inequalities are necessary as incentives – that if you want to motivate people to work longer hours, or to concentrate harder, or to change to a different job, you have to offer them a financial inducement. But how much do you have to offer them? That's not an easy question to answer, but it might be possible to get a rough general picture by looking at pay schemes currently in use.

Think for example of overtime work. It's quite common for overtime to be paid at no more than one-and-a-half times basic pay; and there doesn't seem to be any shortage of people willing to take it. At that rate, working 10 per cent longer than usual gets you 15 per cent more income. In 1984, about half of the manual workers in Britain received overtime pay; it got them about 17 per cent more income for 12 per cent more work. In piecework and bonus schemes, workers are paid according to output, sometimes only after they've exceeded a certain quota. Often such schemes raise your pay in direct proportion to your output, and it's rare for them to offer more than about 12 per cent more pay for 10 per cent more production. In Britain about 45 per cent of manual workers were on bonus schemes in 1984, and bonuses accounted for about 9 per cent of their earnings.

The general conclusion these figures suggest is that people seem quite willing to work an extra 10 per cent longer or harder for an increased pay of 15 per cent or less. At that rate, you could get people to work twice as hard as average for about two and a half times the average wage. But is any job – airline pilot, company director, stockbroker, banker – really twice as hard as the work done by a typical manual worker? That's a matter of judgment on which no 'scientific' study is going to be much use; in my own personal judgment, I doubt that there is, but you can put in your own guess and change the figures accordingly. On my guess, it seems reasonable to suppose that sufficient incentives would exist even if no one were paid more than about two and a half times the average manual wage.

If all this guesswork is anywhere near the truth, then pay differentials as they stand are much greater than are needed for incentives. In particular, well-paid executives and 'pro-fessionals' could be paid a lot less without any risk of being lured away to teaching or brick-laying or typing. This conclusion is strengthened by looking at some cross-national comparisons. For instance, a 1975 study showed that the basic salary of a typical general manager for a large company in France was more than five and a half times that of someone at the level of line supervisor. In the UK, the multiple was three and a third, while in Australia it was only two and a half. If a 150 per cent gap is big enough to get Australians to climb the corporate ladder, why shouldn't it be big enough to motivate French people?

In a capitalist economy, the main factors determining high incomes are economic power and scarcity. Economic power, in that top managers can often fix their own pay without outside interference; scarcity, in that managerial and 'professional' talent may be in short supply and big demand. Both factors go beyond the problem of motivating people to work, to questions about the power structure of capitalist firms and the role of markets. Some of these questions are taken up later in this chapter, as well as in other parts of this book. The point here is that the incentive argument on its own can only account for a relatively narrow range of income.

Incentives and equality

Suppose we had a system in which democratic planning and income taxes limited income differentials to whatever was needed for incentives. How different would that be from a genuinely egalitarian pay structure? Well, Chapter 6 discussed the idea of a 'compensating differential'. That's the difference in pay and conditions between two kinds or degrees of work which makes them roughly equally attractive. And it was argued that those differentials would be perfectly justified in an egalitarian society. My guess there was that compensating differentials might themselves range up to about twice the average income. So just on the basis of subjective guesses, it doesn't look like 'incentive' differentials would have to be very different from compensating ones.

It's no accident that these two pieces of guesswork should largely coincide. For if differentials were merely compensating, people would have no incentive to choose one kind of work rather than another. Thus, in general, incentive differentials might have to be a little more or a little less than compensating ones. It's that 'little more' or 'little less' that tells you the maximum range of real inequality justified by the incentive argument: not a lot, in the end, to get very excited about!

It's a *maximum* range, because another factor might make even those small inequalities unnecessary. For even in a strictly egalitarian economy, where all differentials were merely compensating, it would be in everyone's interest to do the most socially useful work open to them. After all, they'd have nothing to *lose* from doing so, since they'd be compensated. And by doing more rather than less useful work, they'd be helping everyone including themselves.

So, strictly speaking, even a fully egalitarian economy would give people an incentive to work. In practice, the idea of a compensating differential is broad enough to make the distinction between a fully egalitarian economy and one with small inequalities purely academic. What's necessary is to develop methods for democratically planning the overall range of incomes and the degree to which markets can be left to operate within those limits. It would be foolish to predict with any precision what distribution of earnings will eventually emerge. The crucial point here is simply that a very substantial degree of equality is completely compatible with incentives.

What Makes People Work?

The last section criticized the incentive argument in its own terms. For the sake of argument, it accepted the assumption that people will only work for the general good if you offer them material inducements to do so, and showed how even that assumption is perfectly compatible with considerable economic equality. But the assumption is obviously false.

Think of the work people do as parents. A 1985 British study showed that women with children spent about fifty hours a week looking after them, not counting the time they just played with them. However complex parents' motives are, it's obvious that they don't do it simply for financial gain. Yet this is one of the most important kinds of work there is.

Think about the work people do for clubs, societies, voluntary organizations, political parties, trade unions. It may be motivated by sheer dedication to the playing of a game, by the need for friendship and a sense of belonging, by a commitment to certain ideals, or maybe by a desire for power or prestige – but it's clear to anyone that people rarely do these things just for money.

Of course, you might admit that all this is true for these 'fringe' activities, but still insist that things are different when it comes to 'real' work – though the distinction between 'fringe' and 'real' is contentious. But is it really true that in people's paid employment it's only money that talks, and that ideas about other kinds of motive are hopelessly idealistic?

Work motivation in the capitalist firm

It may come as a surprise to learn that the people who study work motivation in capitalist firms, and who train capitalist managers, are among the strongest critics of a money-only mentality. Management textbooks discussing rival theories of motivation recognize that making people work is a complicated business. People work not just for money, but for other reasons, too: such as the satisfactions they get from using their skills, the sense of achievement this gives them, the companionship and esteem of fellow workers, the status their work gives them in the community. Workers can be motivated by making their jobs more interesting, by better working conditions, by more participation in management, by being praised and recognized for their accomplishments. Even in the area of income, many management textbooks stress that the important thing is not so much that pay be tied to production in a 'carrot and stick' way, as that it be related to people's work in a way recognized by everyone as 'fair'. So even money motivation operates through people's moral beliefs about fairness in a manner simply ignored by the crude incentive arguments discussed earlier.

Naturally, textbooks for capitalist managers don't bite the hand that feeds them. They don't draw the conclusion that their findings on motivation make a radically different social structure both possible and desirable. For the very basis of the capitalist firm prevents the full use of just those motivating factors which they recognize as important. In particular, it prevents the extension of workers' democracy into the area of managerial control. When such participation as the capitalist firm allows is recognized as only an illusion of influence, its motivational benefits are likely to vanish. These built-in limits to workers' participation also restrict the capitalist firm's ability to make jobs more satisfying, since a greater power over your job is a key form of job enrichment.

Capitalism places out of reach any stable and significant motivation through teamwork and commitment to the firm, since the firm is evidently *not* a team but a power structure in which labour works *for* capital. The point is not that workers have no material interest in the success of the firm, since of course they do. With or without profit-sharing deals, their incomes will tend to reflect the firm's overall performance. The point is that the further, non-material motives which derive from identifying with the firm as a social unit are at best fragile accommodations based on a deceit. Even the cosiest capitalist firm is soon seen for what it is when a change in the economic climate leads to closures and redundancies.

Finally, capitalist firms can never make full use of the idea of fairness in setting their wage rates. Of course, they can and do engage in job evaluation schemes designed to establish 'fair' differentials among their employees. But they cannot risk opening up too critical a discussion of inequalities of pay, or prevent job evaluation schemes from being tainted by their obvious exclusion of the incomes of top managers, directors, and shareholders. For suppose workers decided that it would be 'fairer' to pay directors less than fitters, or shareholders less than typists: where would capitalism be then?

Thus, ironically, capitalist 'management science' provides some of the strongest motivational arguments you can find for the abolition of capitalism itself.

The experience of non-capitalist systems

The programme of extending non-income motivation beyond the limits of capitalism is not an idle dream. It has already been tried in the real world. Like most complicated experience, its lessons aren't simple and direct, but it does throw light on the possibilities.

One obvious area of experience is the small but growing number of industrial co-ops. Firms are built on principles of democratic management, limited or no pay differentials, job flexibility, and motivation by commitment to the group and a sense of mutual responsibility. The number of co-ops in Britain trebled from 1980 to 1984, and there are now over 900 co-ops with over 20,000 people working in them. An estimated 750-1000 co-ops are doing business in the US.

Many British co-ops face serious financial problems stemming largely from under-investment, but they certainly don't suffer from lack of motivation. To be sure, the motivation is *partly* financial, but of precisely the egalitarian kind discussed in the last section – everyone gains equally from a co-op's success. But money is rarely the only reason people join. They also want the benefits a money-only mentality ignores – control over their work, job satisfaction, and a sense of community.

The largest European co-operative group was founded at Mondragon in Spain in 1956. By the early 1980s it consisted of over 80 industrial co-ops with more than 18,000 members. The range of incomes is very compressed, with the highest paid members receiving only 4.5 times as much as the lowest paid. Everyone has a financial stake in the firm through credits to and deductions from individual investment accounts that are cashed in when a member leaves. But a study of Mondragon showed that its workers also place a high value on cooperative working as such: 71 per cent said that they would not change jobs even for a 50 per cent pay rise. Major motivating factors include greater control over one's job and a greater participation in important decisions. Managers are accountable to the workforce and are replaced if incompetent. As a result, members have a very different view of the relationship between managers and workers from the view that prevails in conventional firms. Work discipline is maintained by collective responsibility instead of hierarchy.

At the moment, co-ops make up only a small part of any western capitalist economy: certainly not enough for us to conclude from them alone that people in general could work for the same kind of motives. What we can conclude is that there is nothing about human nature or western culture or modern technology which makes cooperative arrangements simply impossible.

A different kind of evidence about why people work comes from those non-capitalist countries which have made extensive use of non-financial motivation, notably China and Cuba. In those countries, the point is usually expressed in terms of the distinction between 'material incentives' and 'moral incentives', though the expressions aren't entirely apt. The phrase 'material incentives' is used to cover any case of paying individuals according to their work, without making any distinction between a compensating differential and a genuine inequality. The category of moral incentives covers everything else – from the provision of collectively provided goods like schools, transport, and clinics, to the awarding of social titles and prizes like 'National Work Hero', to programmes of job enrichment and workers' participation, to popular campaigns for higher production or a big sugar harvest. Obviously, these motivational devices work in rather different ways. Providing schools and hospitals is material, but collective and egalitarian. Medals and titles operate through public praise and prestige. Job enrichment and participation operate through the attractiveness of people's work. Popular campaigns are based on public spirit and a sense of community. But none of these relies on the simple motive of more money for more work.

It would be nice to be able to say whether Cuba and China prove or disprove that we could adopt moral incentives on a national scale. Unfortunately the issue isn't so simple. For one thing, analysts of their economies strongly disagree about the extent and effectiveness of moral incentives, a disagreement which almost certainly can't be resolved because there are so many other factors affecting their overall economic performance. One crucial difference between their situation and ours is that they are much poorer countries, and have had to concentrate on building an economic base which we (at least until recently) could take for granted. But in any case, their use of moral incentives faces limits very similar to those operating in capitalist firms. Management remains hierarchical, with important decisions being handed down from above rather than democratically determined. Such participation as exists is expected to endorse the Party line and to facilitate the Party's objectives. The conflict of interest between bureaucratic elites and ordinary workers limits the potential for appeals to teamwork and community. Income differentials, though narrower than in capitalist countries, are bureaucratically determined, as are the privileges afforded to administrators. The Cuban and Chinese economies are thus themselves unable to make full use of moral incentives, and have recently paid more attention to the material.

So what's the point in mentioning them? It's that for all the difficulties of analysing and evaluating their experience, they still provide the most serious attempt in a modern economy to rely on non-material motives. It would be unwise to deny either that they've made costly mistakes which required changes or that they've exposed new possibilities. We can learn from them if we have a mind to.

The lessons for us

Try to imagine an annual award called 'National Work Hero of Britain'. Pretty unlikely, isn't it? We are so used to living in a society where most work is pointless, soul-destroying, subservient, and dominated by a fundamental conflict of interest between employers and workers, that it's hard to conceive of giving workers the kind of recognition we now reserve for entrepreneurs, entertainers, and sports stars. But in the findings of management consultants, in the experiences of workers' co-ops, in the experiments of China and Cuba, we can dimly see the elements of a different picture of working and living, in which *of course* we'd still have to work in order to live, but in which no one need say that they 'only do it for the money'. Even if it's a picture which life may never fully live up to, it is an understandable ideal which can guide our political choices.

The issue of this chapter is a little more down to earth than that grand image. It concerns the question: does society benefit from inequalities? In particular, these last two sections have discussed whether societies need substantial inequalities to motivate people. The first part of the answer was that even in its own terms, the incentive argument is consistent with substantial economic equality. The second part of the answer is that everyone knows that there are other motives besides material gain – many of which gather strength precisely in situations of greater material equality. Neither of these answers proves conclusively that an egalitarian society would be as productive as an unequal one, but they do cast doubt on the conventional view to the contrary. An egalitarian society would also provide people with more satisfying jobs, more control over their work, more sense of purpose, more fellow feeling, and popular control over the distribution of income – kinds of benefit which the incentive argument ignores. Wouldn't such a society gain more from its equality than inequality could ever bring?

'The Dead Hand of Bureaucracy'

Would an egalitarian society stagger under the weight of bureaucratic mismanagement? That's a popular image of socialism, reinforced by welfare bureaucracies at home and by reports of life in eastern Europe. Critics say that since egalitarians admit that they're socialists, and since socialism is inevitably bureaucratic, equality must surely be costly to society as a whole. Society would be better off with less bureaucracy but more inequality.

Is that argument any good? To evaluate it, it helps to distinguish between two types of bureaucracy with which socialism is associated – welfare bureaucracies and planning bureaucracies.

Welfare bureaucracies

A lot of the most criticized waste and inefficiency in our society is within the welfare bureaucracies – the health service, the social security system, public housing, social work, education, community relations. Yet these are just the sorts of organization that egalitarian socialists support. Does that prove that socialism equals bureaucracy equals waste?

Well, socialists are committed to satisfying people's needs. They argue that the capitalist economy is incapable of doing this. Within capitalist economies, most socialists have promoted welfare bureaucracies as a way of relieving capitalism's worst effects. But that doesn't mean they have to condone bureaucratic waste. If inefficiency in these organizations means worse provision for needs, then to criticize it is to take an egalitarian position. It's to take the side of the *users* of these services against bad design and management. Socialists are likely to offer a different explanation of waste, and a different cure, from those given by their opponents – blaming it on paternalistic, undemocratic structures, and ultimately on the role of welfare bureaucracies in a capitalist society, rather than on the fact that bureaucracies don't have to make a profit. They can also recognize the social cost of reducing public employment in the midst of an economic depression. But the *principle* on which bureaucratic waste is condemned is an egalitarian one; if needs really can be provided for with less waste, egalitarians can only approve.

The same point holds for the issue of welfare bureaucracies in a socialist society. As it happens, socialists disagree among themselves about the role of direct administrative provision for need in a socialist economy, with some advocating much more use of markets than others. We will return to this dispute about 'market socialism' in a moment. But the principle that needs should be provided for as efficiently as possible is simply the principle that resources should be used to benefit everyone instead of being wasted.

So on the question of welfare bureaucracies, there is simply no argument for connecting egalitarians with bureaucratic waste. The real issues are over the best *institutions* for satisfying needs – bureaus or firms, integrated or competing, centralized or localized. These are important questions for egalitarians, but not the issues of principle which this book is about.

Planning bureaucracies

Most egalitarians believe that equality could only be achieved in a democratically planned economy: that is, an economy in which major questions about investment, production, and the distribution of incomes are consciously decided through a democratic political process. Such planning is necessary to abolish unemployment and poverty, to make work satisfying and stimulating, to put decisions under democratic control, to make incomes more equal, to do away with discrimination and exploitation. But doesn't such planning also create a massive bureaucratic machine? More waste, more inefficiency, more of a burden for society as a whole?

If the argument is simply about bureaucratic waste – red tape, botched decisions, inflexibility and incompetence – then it is an argument perfectly compatible with egalitarianism. All these forms of waste are ways in which the pursuit of equality can be in one way or another slowed down or undermined. Thus egalitarians have as much at stake in finding ways of avoiding such waste as anyone else. As with the issue of welfare bureaucracies, *this* criticism is on the side of equality, not against it.

The real issue between equality and its critics is not over the *efficiency* with which planning bureaucracies might achieve their aims, but over the cost to society of planning itself. Critics argue that even an efficiently organized plan of the size and complexity necessary for achieving equality would be very expensive to produce and implement. It would be such a burden on society that everyone would be better off with less planning, even if this meant less equality. Here at last we have a real benefit-all argument against equality. Is it right?

Replying to this argument raises some big questions of social and economic policy; all I intend to do here is to sketch out the basic form of that reply. It has two stages. The first stage is to show that even at the level of satisfying everyone's basic needs, a planned economy is better than an unplanned economy. The second stage is to ask how much additional planning would really be necessary to implement the other principles of equality. That will reveal not so much the validity of the benefit-all argument as its importance.

Full-blooded defenders of capitalism assert that a free market economy is better at satisfying needs than even the most mildly planned one. They are no-planning extremists, although even they recognize the need for individual businesses to plan, and for the government to plan for some basic common services. But hardly anyone believes in that position. If you look at the policies of the Thatcher government, for example, you find a substantial amount of economic planning, aimed at a reduced public sector, support for private investors, low inflation, and other objectives which benefit big business. A more egalitarian attitude towards planning is found among 'social democrats'. They believe that governments should try to protect the weakest members of society by using taxation, government spending, consultation with business organizations and trade unions, employment legislation, regulations on quality and pollution, and similar policies of the sort used extensively in capitalist countries since the 1930s. In criticism, socialists point out that this sort of government planning leaves major issues concerning investment and production under private control, and they argue that in such a system it's impossible to satisfy everyone's basic needs.

The socialist case has been put on many occasions, but some of the central arguments are these. First of all, capitalism always seems to require poverty. In the richest countries there are people still homeless or living in slums, still dying of cold in the winter, still malnourished and badly clothed. Yet these countries obviously have the resources to eliminate poverty altogether. So why don't they? Well, capitalist economies operate by means of private investment for profit. Without the prospect of making a profit, capitalists would not invest. But profits can only exist if wages are kept under control. So capitalism needs to ensure that they are. Wages in a capitalist economy are set by the relative bargaining strength of workers and employers. And the most effective way of limiting the bargaining strength of workers is the threat of unemployment and poverty – a threat which gets its force from the actual presence of the poor and unemployed.

Capitalist economies have sometimes used other ways to keep wages down, for instance government wage restraint. But this manner of *planning* wages runs into a problem of democracy: it needs the participation of trade unions to make it work, but takes place in the midst of a deeply undemocratic economy. For most capitalist economies, for most of the time, nothing really works like poverty. Capitalism can't afford to pay unemployed workers decently – not because of 'recession', but because it *needs* them to be poor. Only a democratically planned economy could plan for full employment.

Not only does capitalism require poverty and unemployment, but its unplanned technical development inevitably *creates* poverty and unemployment. In the competitive market, firms have a constant interest in finding cheaper forms of production – ways of decreasing the costs of production, and thus increasing profit. Throughout its history, capitalism has demonstrated again and again how this can be done by substituting machinery for workers, from steam engines to computers. Sometimes existing firms replace their own workers; sometimes new, more mechanized firms drive old firms out of business. Either way, the net effect is people out of work, for longer or shorter spells, until the unplanned development of the economy creates new forms of employment. Technical change also changes the geography of capitalism, throwing whole communities out of work, forcing people to move, shifting the centres of prosperity and poverty.

Attempts have been made to soften the effects of technical change within capitalist countries by subsidizing industry, restricting imports, setting up regional funds and retraining schemes, and so on. They're simply no match for the remorseless force of the capitalist economy. Only a democratically planned economy with investment under social control could introduce technical change in ways that avoided these enormous social costs.

Besides its inability to satisfy people's basic material needs, capitalism frustrates many other needs. Needs for autonomy and self-development, needs for fulfilment and creativity, needs for community, security, dignity, privacy, self-respect. Profitability controls both work and leisure, production and consumption. Only a democratically planned economy could pay attention to those needs which don't figure on a company's balance sheet.

Now if only a democratically planned economy is capable of satisfying everyone's basic needs, then the benefit-all argument against planning costs is at least partly defeated. No one can argue that everyone would be better off in a capitalist economy than in a planned one. But a planned economy which satisfied everyone's needs might not yet be a fully equal one. It might take more extensive planning, with greater administrative costs, to achieve equality. So everyone might still be better off with less planning and more inequality.

That's a benefit-all argument which many socialists agree with. They argue that the only way to avoid the massive costs of a fully planned economy is to rely to a certain extent on market mechanisms. Instead of gathering complicated information about who wants what and sending out complicated instructions about who should produce it, planners should leave individual shops and manufacturing units to respond to the supply and demand of the market. The system would be socialist, because firms would be worker-managed, the major means of production would be socially owned, and the overall shape and direction of the economy would be democratically planned. But it would be a market socialism.

The question posed by the idea of market socialism is simply this: to what extent does an economy have to choose between greater equality and lower planning costs? Market socialists usually admit that their policies would produce some inequalities, but argue that the inequalities needn't be very big. (The argument partly depends on assumptions about motivation of the sort discussed in previous sections.) Advocates of greater planning usually admit that their policies would involve some costs but deny that less planning would benefit everyone. Of course, the fact that neither side thinks that you have to choose between equality and lower planning costs doesn't show that you don't. After all, each side denies the other's confident reassurances! But market socialists agree that major questions of investment and production would need to be planned, and advocates of greater planning agree that you can't plan everything. So perhaps, in the end, the benefit-all argument that the costs of planning justify market-created inequalities may not be very important. Perhaps some combination of planning and markets would be *reasonably* equal. But to argue for that in detail is more than it's in the scope of this book to do. Readers who want to pursue the matter can start at 'References and Further Reading'.

Does Democracy Cost Too Much?

Egalitarians believe not just in economic equality, but in political equality, too: in giving people equal power over the decisions affecting their lives. That principle implies a tremendous extension of democracy, in government, the economy, education, family life, and other social institutions. But isn't there a benefit-all argument against this? Wouldn't everyone be worse off in that ultra-democratic world than they are now?

The benefit-all argument for political inequality could rely on three different premises. First of all, that extensive democracy is just *inefficient* – it takes too much time and energy. Secondly, that full-scale democracy is *incompetent* – that ordinary people simply do not and cannot know everything you need to know to make sensible decisions. Thirdly, that widespread democracy is *indecisive* – it generates so much conflict that nothing serious ever gets done. None of these premises denies the value of a moderate, representative democracy, in which people who for the most part know what they're doing are elected to Parliament, boards of management, local councils, and specialist committees, or appointed by such bodies, and allowed to get on with the job. What they object to is leaving the decision to interminable, incompetent mass meetings.

The basic egalitarian response to these arguments is to insist that having increased control over your life is generally a benefit of greater value than the costs involved in exercising that control. And so it's not true that people are better off with less democracy than with more. People benefit from being involved in decisions not just because the results are more likely to suit them, but also because self-determination is itself valuable. When the benefit-all argument for limited democracy says that participation costs too much, it's neglecting the benefit of participation itself.

There may be times and circumstances when this response doesn't hold – for instance, when the value of self-determination has to be overridden by the value of mere survival. This is arguably true of a crisis produced by a famine, epidemic, natural disaster, or war. It's possible, too, that in extremely poor countries everyone could be made better off by more production and less discussion, though the choice doesn't

necessarily arise. But for our own society, there is a strong
case for more democracy even at a cost.

But who's to judge? Who says that more self-determination
is worth the cost? As a piece of argument, it is open to
egalitarians to maintain this on the strength of their own
experience, their observations, and their beliefs about human
wellbeing. As a political programme, it has to be subjected,
like all other political programmes, to the test of democratic
choice. The ultimate proof that participation is worth the cost
is that people choose to participate. What, then, are we to say
about the fact that in our own society most people *don't* take
part in politics?

Good design

The costs and benefits of participation depend a lot on
circumstances. People whose lives are ground down by poverty
and exhausting work, and whose education has done nothing
to develop their critical faculties, find it hard to summon up
the energy to discuss, reflect, listen, and evaluate in the way
that active participation involves. And if the forms of
participation available are boring, tedious, time-consuming,
and trivial, it's no wonder if nobody takes part. We all know
people who enjoy going to meetings, who are happy to argue
about anything, however unimportant, who love the sound of
their own voices. But democracy is not a sport. If we value
participation, it has to be based on the fact that the decisions
taken actually matter.

An egalitarian society would have to take a serious interest
in the design of decision-making, aiming to minimize the costs
of participation and to maximize self-determination. The
forms now used in political parties, trade unions, and pressure
groups are obviously inadequate for these tasks. Anyone who
blames the members of an organization for their lack of
commitment is looking in the wrong direction – the problem is
to change the organization itself so that participation has more
meaning.

But more participation doesn't have to mean more and
more mass meetings. There's nothing wrong in principle about
delegating decisions to representatives and committees. Even
five people in a democratic household can't talk everything out
– should Dave buy beans tomorrow if the price goes up by a
penny? They have to trust each other to make decisions

knowing each others' tastes and opinions. In a larger, more complicated system, it makes sense to delegate a lot of decisions, to mark out wider areas of trust, and to formalize them in representative institutions. In a sense, that process gives some people more power than others, but only in a sense. If it was a democratic choice to delegate decisions in the first place, if the representatives in question are expected to choose in line with the known views of their constituents and to give a full account of their actions, and if the group can withdraw this power and censure its holders in any case of misconduct, it's a little odd to call it an inequality at all. And whatever you call it, there doesn't seem to be anything about it that egalitarians have to disagree with.

Knowledge

Good design, including delegated responsibilities, is a way of reducing the costs and increasing the benefits of participation, but it doesn't in itself deal with the charge of incompetence. Critics argue that it's all very well giving the residents of Happy Families Estate control over whether the lamp posts will be black or green: it's quite another matter to consult them about designing the computer system in Town Hall. It's fine, they say, to give the ordinary workers in Useful Enterprise PLC the decision over when to take their tea break, but you can't expect them to decide questions about production, marketing, forward planning, and investment. Those are matters for experts, not for the common people.

But democracy doesn't require people to be experts on everything. It merely requires that experts be forced to submit their recommendations to genuine public scrutiny. The decisions now taken about computer installations in Town Halls are reviewed by committees who are not all computer experts, but who are still capable of understanding general information about what different systems can do, how much they cost, and how they'll affect the Town Hall's work. There's no reason why the residents of Happy Families Estate shouldn't be involved in that kind of activity by having easy and regular access to information and the right to raise questions and initiate objections.

The same argument applies in business. The directors of capitalist companies are not all experts in the details of production, marketing, planning, and investment, but that doesn't prevent them from taking what they confidently believe to be competent managerial decisions. There's no reason why at least the same degree of competence shouldn't be displayed by the democratically elected boards of worker-managed companies, or why they shouldn't be able to account fully for their decisions to the people who elected them.

Naturally, a widespread shift to participatory democracy would depend on ordinary people coming to know and understand a lot of things about the world that they do not know or understand now. For instance, research has shown time and again that the citizens of western democracies have only the faintest knowledge of the policies and personalities of major political parties. But why should they? They have correspondingly little power. In a more democratic society, in which you were involved in decisions that actually mattered to your life, you would have a reason to know what was going on. And the experience of participation would itself improve your ability to handle the kinds of issues you would have to deal with.

Conflict

Finally, there's the issue of whether too much democracy creates too much conflict, resulting in either a stagnant lack of decisiveness or widespread and dangerous disaffection. Strong, effective government seems to need a certain freedom of manoeuvre, a certain distance from the conflicts and pressures of different social groupings. This objection has no simple answer. Deeply divided societies really are difficult to govern; greater public participation does put representatives under more pressure; heightened social conflict can be destabilizing.

But one thing is obvious – that greater equality is likely to decrease the amount of social division, and so improve the prospects for effective democratic government. An egalitarian society which provided economic security, personal respect, and a sense of community would have far less social conflict than our own. People wouldn't think of politics as a dog-eat-dog world in which groups struggled to protect their interests. There would be a greater sense of common interest and mutual benefit. Politics would be less concerned with arbitrating conflicts than with deciding what we'd like to do together. Participatory democracy can be effective, but only in a more equal society.

Thus the benefit-all argument against political equality is a failure. But it is also a challenge. For it only fails if egalitarians can use their skill and imagination to develop forms of participation which really increase people's power over their own lives, through good design and an extension of competence. It's a challenge which most egalitarians could take a lot more seriously than they have in the past.

What Economics Doesn't Prove

Benefit-all arguments are complicated and resilient. Here are some additional examples, starting with economics and moving on to democracy.

There surely is a conflict between equality and efficiency, because – as anyone who's done a little economics can tell you – a free market is perfectly efficient.

What people who have done a little economics know is that 'perfect competition' is said by economics books to be 'efficient'. As an argument against equality, that counts for just about nothing.

The first reason it counts for just about nothing is that no capitalist country operates on the basis of perfect competition. That's not just because of the degree of government intervention in the economy – much of that intervention was a direct response to 'market imperfections'. The most important of these imperfections, as anyone who's done a little more economics can tell you, are the domination of many markets by a few large firms, the fact that market transactions produce side-effects like pollution, and the ignorance and gullibility of consumers.

The second reason it counts for just about nothing is that what economics books mean by 'efficient' has just about no importance on its own. They mean that *given* a certain distribution of resources and *given* the desires, however created, of consumers, market transactions will lead to an 'equilibrium' at which no further transaction will make anyone better off without making someone else worse off. For instance, some people may still want to sell their labour for a living wage, but no one may want to buy it at that price. The perfect efficiency of the perfect market is entirely compatible with mass poverty.

In fact, efficiency is always a question of how effectively a machine or system achieves certain ends, and is only as important as the ends themselves are. In this chapter, the discussion of bureaucracy assumes that the aim of satisfying everyone's basic needs is an important end, and therefore that it is important to pursue this end efficiently. The aim of achieving a market equilibrium is not, on its own, a very important end; hence the efficiency of markets in achieving it is only of secondary importance.

Maybe people would have an incentive to work in an egalitarian society, but how could there be any incentive to invest? Isn't that just as serious a problem?

In a capitalist economy, the incentive to invest is profit, and increasing it means increasing the income of the private individuals and firms who control capital. That's why the incentive to invest is so popular with Conservative politicians. But a country's investment doesn't have to be organized this way. In a socialist economy, private investment would be at most a minor factor. The investment of socially controlled wealth would be aimed at benefiting everyone, and this benefit to everyone would act as an incentive. Working out in detail the best institutions for making investments is not at all simple. The point here is only that encouraging investment in a socialist economy is a very different problem from encouraging it under capitalism.

Democracy may benefit everyone, but surely it may not. Suppose for instance that a majority oppresses a minority, as the unionists have done to catholics in Northern Ireland. Surely that's a valid argument against democracy.

The central principle of democracy is political equality: the principle of equal power. Majority rule is often an appropriate way of instituting the principle, since in general it can be thought of as giving everyone an equal say in the decisions affecting them. But majority rule isn't sacrosanct. When a majority uses its power to make a minority powerless, the general connection between majority rule and political equality is broken. In such a case, new institutions have to be devised, and the principle for devising them remains egalitarian. It is that people should as far as possible exercise equal power over their lives. If majority rule can't achieve that, then the principle of democracy itself calls for a different system.

9

Is Equality Possible?

The opponents of equality sometimes object that however much people *ought* to be equal, they aren't and never will be. Equality is just an idle dream. For if equality were possible, why are we surrounded by inequality? Why has there never been an egalitarian society? Why have egalitarian movements always failed?

In one form, the objection is perfectly sound. Nobody with any sense of reality can believe that societies can be planned to perfection, that somehow you could eradicate every social evil, inegalitarian or otherwise. This objection applies to almost any social ideal. But it's simply a misunderstanding of the point of having ideals and standards in the first place to complain that reality can never fully live up to them. There will of course always be inequalities inasmuch as social institutions will always have imperfections which some people will take advantage of. That's not a serious objection to equality at all.

The real issue concerns the big, important inequalities which are so marked in our own and every other modern society. If even they were impossible to get rid of, egalitarianism really would be in trouble.

This chapter looks at some of the most common arguments for the claim that inequalities of that scale are unavoidable, and shows that the arguments are unconvincing. Nobody has proved that equality is impossible. A key idea in the discussion is that inequality is not a direct outcome of an unchanging *human nature*, but depends on the way *social structures* shape human nature and regulate human relationships. Social structures have changed in the past and will change in the future. The difficult question is whether there's any hope of changing them in an egalitarian direction.

'But People *Aren't* Equal!'

Look at the world around you and everywhere you see inequalities. Any two people you choose are likely to differ not just physically, but in their desires, abilities, and characters. One is ambitious, another content. One is a brilliant musician, another mediocre. One is friendly and generous, another aggressive and dishonest. People *aren't* equal – how can anyone imagine that they could be?

Though this is a familiar objection with a strong air of common sense, it involves a simple mistake. Egalitarianism doesn't aim to make people equal in their personal character- istics: it isn't committed to everyone being the same. On the contrary, egalitarians argue for a society in which each person can express her or his own individuality, however uncon- ventional. So it's actually more likely that equality will bring out personal differences rather than repress them. These differences – a better word for them than 'inequalities' – are likely to exist in any society, but they're not on equality's hit list.

People are now unequal in many other ways. In particular, some live in luxury while others starve; some control great power and wealth while others are poor and oppressed; some enjoy honour and deference while others suffer degradation and contempt. Egalitarians do oppose these inequalities. But it's no defence of *these* inequalities to say that people aren't equal in these ways. Everyone knows that they aren't – what's not at all obvious is that they have to be.

So it's important to remember to distinguish between the inequalities egalitarianism accepts and those it rejects. That distinction matches, to a large extent, the common-sense contrast between the inequalities which seem to be part of the human condition and those which seem open to change. If you want to show that equality's impossible, you have to go beyond that common-sense distinction, and show that the inequalities of wealth, power, and status which look changeable really aren't. That requires a lot more argument than just asserting that people aren't equal. In general, it requires you to explain why such inequalities exist, and why they can't be done away with. The rest of this chapter looks at some common attempts to do just that.

Is Inequality in our Nature?

The most popular explanation of inequality is probably that it's part of 'human nature'. It's only natural that people should want to be rich and powerful and famous; given their unequal abilities, it's only natural that some should end up better off than others. According to this view, equality is only on the agenda if people can be turned from ordinary human beings into angels who no longer care about their own interests – and that, of course, is impossible.

It's a plausible argument. Certainly, its general view of what people are like seems to be proved by everyday experience. To be sure, there are a few examples even in our own society of genuine equality – some families, some communes, some religious and political groups. But these look like the exceptions that prove the rule: that, in general, people are too selfish and too ambitious for equality.

But everyday experience can be deceptive. First of all, it may only be telling you that you can never have perfect equality. Somebody will always be able to get a little more power or wealth or prestige than somebody else; there will always be petty hierarchies, squabbles, winners and losers. As we've seen, that's no objection at all. Egalitarians are concerned with the major, structured inequalities which frustrate needs, undermine respect, destroy community and restrict freedom, not with getting rid of every single case of personal advantage.

Secondly, it's wrong for objectors to imagine that exceptions to inequality are also exceptions to self-interest. Even the most purely egalitarian kibbutz operates on the basis that everyone benefits from participating. Nobody is expected to be a martyr: to do nothing but give, never to receive. On the contrary, each member benefits both materially and in other ways, such as by having greater job satisfaction, more control over their work, and more respect from others. But the structure of the kibbutz means that you can only benefit yourself by acting in ways which benefit others, too. The same thing applies in other examples of equality, like working in a co-op, living in an egalitarian household, or belonging to a self-help group like Alcoholics Anonymous. In each case, there's a *social structure* which links helping yourself with helping others.

The third problem with everyday experience is that it tends to make things which are in fact peculiar to our own society look as if they're just human nature. The fact is that every society shapes human beings in various ways, bringing out some feelings more strongly than others, rewarding some forms of action and punishing others. The great inequalities of our own society both determine and reinforce the forms it gives to selfishness and ambition, so that, for instance, it is considered more attractive and even more honest to satisfy your ambition by making a lot of money than by being a social worker. In a different society, self-interest and ambition might have a very different appearance and might be very much less likely on their own to lead inevitably to inequality.

If equality doesn't really depend on people being angels, and if societies can shape people's natures in a variety of ways, then maybe human nature is compatible with equality after all. But is there any positive evidence to believe that it is? Perhaps the best evidence comes from research done by anthropologists on societies whose members live by foraging, gathering wild plant foods and hunting animals. Unlike the examples of co-ops, communes, and kibbutzim, their life could hardly be called an experiment: it is in all probability typical of the ways in which whole societies ordered their affairs for hundreds of generations. So no one could consider these peoples to be exceptions to human nature, even if they're now very rare.

Foraging societies vary in structure, but some of the most carefully studied of them are strongly egalitarian. A good example is provided by the !Kung San people in southern Africa. (The '!' stands for a tongue click.) The !Kung have been studied by many anthropologists, including a major research project operating from Harvard from 1963 to 1976. They live in semi-nomadic 'camps' of ten to seventy people. Their customs concerning the distribution of both gathered and hunted food ensure that everyone is equally well fed. Their major resource, the land they live in, is communally controlled; no one accumulates much more strictly private property (tools, clothing, ornaments) than anyone else, and even these are expected to be shared. In short, they have *systems of property* which preserve equality. Although camps have informal patterns of leadership, no one has any formal power over other members. There are conflicts, of course, sometimes culminating in fights; but in general conflict is resolved by discussion, and in the last resort by splitting the camp. A major sexual division occurs in !Kung society, since women do most of the gathering and men all of the big game hunting, but relations between the sexes are kept on a broadly equal basis.

An obvious problem in a culture relying on hunting skill is how to prevent good hunters from dominating everyone else. The !Kung teach them to be modest about their accomplishments, and refuse to make a big show of gratitude. A !Kung man explained:

> Say that a man has been hunting. He must not come home and announce like a braggart, 'I have killed a big one in the bush!' He must first sit down in silence until I or someone else comes up to his fire and asks, 'What did you see today?' He replies quietly, 'Ah, I'm no good for hunting. I saw nothing at all . . . maybe just a tiny one.' Then I smile to myself because I now know he has killed something big.

When they go to pick up the kill, people say things like: 'You mean to say you have dragged us all the way out here to make us cart home your pile of bones? Oh, if I had known it was this thin I wouldn't have come.' The hunter is expected to be self-demeaning. As another man explained, these practices 'cool his heart and make him gentle'.

The !Kung are human beings like the rest of us, with likes and dislikes, different personalities, and the capacity for selfishness and pride. Yet they live a relatively peaceful, egalitarian way of life. They are not a model of egalitarianism – nobody's arguing that we should all become hunter-gatherers. But they confirm the conclusion that it isn't human nature that prevents equality. To explain what causes in-equality, and so to discover whether a society like ours can hope for an egalitarian future, you have to bring in more than human nature. You have to look at the nature of human societies, and at how different social structures promote or discourage equality. That question is taken up in a moment, following a brief look at the particular way human nature arguments have been used against women.

Will Men Always Dominate Women?

Thanks to the women's movement, more and more people doubt whether male dominance is really natural and inevitable. Feminist writers have provided a tremendous amount of intellectual support for their position, and if you want to examine their case in detail you can start at 'References and Further Reading'. But the basic argument is worth restating, and it emphasizes some of the more general points just made.

The argument that male dominance is inevitable has two major steps. The first step is to assert that men and women are naturally different ('unequal') in certain specific ways. Obviously men and women have different reproductive capacities, but many other differences have been asserted, such as differences in body chemistry, intelligence, brain structure, and so on. Since nobody can pretend that men and women are *naturally* different in power, income, wealth, or status, the argument needs a second step, which asserts that the 'natural inequalities' inevitably lead to these important 'social inequalities'. For instance, that men's superior strength leads to their having power over women; or that men's superior rationality puts them into positions of leadership.

Whenever you try to fill in the details, at least one of the steps goes badly wrong. The most obvious problem is that the closer you stick to clear, provable differences between men and women in Step 1, the harder it is to pretend in Step 2 that these differences have to create inequalities. For instance, women do clearly and beyond doubt get pregnant and have babies. But there is no direct link between having babies and being dominated – both the Queen and Margaret Thatcher are mothers, but they have achieved the pinnacles of wealth, status, and political power.

So believers in male dominance have to move Step 1 of the argument cautiously away from such obvious differences, to weaker, more contentious claims. Like the claim that women in general, and on average, are less 'aggressive' than men, or think in a less 'logical' way. These differences at least *look* as though they could account for male dominance. But proving that they exist is much harder. Terms like 'aggression' are hard to apply in different social contexts; it's hard to distinguish aggressive behaviour from the dominance it's supposed to explain; apparent counter-examples need to be explained away; it's hard not to project the particular characteristics of your own culture onto human nature itself.

Only a case by case criticism of theories of natural sex differences could actually demonstrate how many of these theories are either false or at least seriously questionable. But anyone who understands what they are trying to do can see the wisdom of approaching them with caution. However much our culture may make us susceptible to their claims, it's sensible to doubt them.

Thus, Step 1 always faces problems. But even if it could be salvaged, the argument would still fail in Step 2 – where male/female differences are supposed to lead to inequalities. For Step 2 is just a special case of the general view that human differences inevitably generate social inequalities, and it falls open to the same general objection. Almost any difference between people could become a basis for inequality in an appropriate social structure. In a warlike society with primitive weapons, physical strength and aggressiveness are going to matter; but they mightn't count for much in a peaceful society. A society geared up for competitive personal advancement won't reward people who are cooperative and caring – and if that society consists of competitive men and cooperative women, then men are likely to end up in its most prominent positions. But this says nothing about how sexual difference might figure in a different social structure.

To illustrate these points, consider again life among the !Kung. Although men and women perform different social roles, the fact that men develop skill in hunting and women in gathering is a division of labour which doesn't become a sex inequality. What's found instead is a complicated set of inequalities which seem roughly to balance out. Women provide more food than men do but with less work, since gathering is more productive than hunting. Yet meat is more highly valued. Women are responsible for young children, but this doesn't prevent them from doing other productive work, and both sexes look after older children and do housework. Neither sex is confined to or excluded from home and family. Marriage and family structure tend if anything to favour women. Camps are based on core groups of both sexes: women are frequently leading members, though apparently less frequently than men. Violence by men against women is much more common than by women against men, but rape is very rare and all violence is strongly condemned. Because the society relies on cooperation and agreement, anyone who is 'naturally' aggressive, dominant, or proud is at a distinct disadvantage.

As before, the purpose of bringing in the !Kung is not to recommend their way of life for us. Sexual equality in our own culture is bound to take a very different form. What the !Kung do show is that human nature doesn't inevitably produce inequality. Any account of the causes of inequality has to consider how human natures interact within human societies and social structures.

Sociological Explanations of Inequality

Whether equality is possible is a matter of possible social structures. Once they get beyond the size and wealth of !Kung society, do they have to be unequal? To answer that question, it helps to have a general theory of inequality – an explanation of why inequality occurs.

As you might expect, there are lots of these theories around, with lots of important differences between them. Fortunately, this chapter is concerned with so broad a question that a very broad distinction between theories of inequality is helpful. The distinction is in terms of a theory's general picture of society, and of the place of inequality within that picture. Following the practice of many sociology textbooks, these can be called the 'functionalist' and 'conflict' views of social inequality.

The 'functionalist' picture of society

Functionalists compare societies to living organisms. In a human body, for instance, there are various organs, each of which performs certain functions contributing to the health and survival of the body as a whole. The same could be said of societies, where different social institutions perform political, religious, economic, educational, and other functions. As in a body, everything works together for the stability and vitality of society as a whole. And as in a body, you can explain something by discovering its function.

This simple picture can be built up into a social theory in a number of ways. But for our broad purposes, it's the basic picture that's important. Our concern is with the kind of explanation this picture provides for inequality, and the implications of this explanation for the future. Why, according to the functionalist view of society, does inequality occur?

The general answer is that inequality performs a social function. It's necessary for social survival and growth. In short, inequality exists because it *benefits society*. But the claim that society benefits from inequality is the very idea criticized in Chapter 8. Functionalist theories are therefore open to the same sorts of criticism. For instance, functionalists argue that every society has to ensure that the right people are attracted to the most important positions. That's why those positions are awarded greater wealth, power, and prestige. But as Chapter 8 demonstrates, a substantially equal society could still motivate people to perform socially useful jobs. It might have to compensate them for differences in difficulty or responsibility, but it needn't employ the major, overall differences of wellbeing which exist in modern societies and which the functionalist theory purports to explain. In any case, there are other forms of motivation besides material gain. All societies rely on these for accomplishing some major tasks, from child care to armed combat. They are, functionally speaking, alternatives to inequality.

Another example of functionalist thinking is the common-place idea that the complexity of modern life requires hierarchies. How could you organize a business or school or bureaucracy or army without a chain of command? Large institutions need a coordinating authority – equality is simply incompatible with their ability to operate.

The answer to that argument is simple, and again relates to a discussion in Chapter 8. It's that there's a distinction between authority and dictatorship. For example, the co-operatives at Mondragon employ managers, who make day to day decisions about the activities of their workforce. What's different is that the managers are democratically accountable to the workers, and are removed if they don't do a satisfactory job. It's a difficult practical problem in any organization to decide just how to structure authority, and a mistaken decision to delegate too much or too little authority can have serious results. But these issues don't undermine the fundamental principle of organizing things democratically. And nobody has yet proved that democracy is fatal.

Neither of these functionalist theories shows that societies need the inequalities they've got. On the contrary, they suggest that societies could function as well or better if they were more egalitarian. So as a basic model for explaining inequality, the functionalist picture of society has to be rejected. And thus, functionalism gives us no compelling reason for believing that equality is impossible. But if inequality can't be explained by the interests of 'society as a whole', the obvious alternative is to explain it in terms of the *part* of society it benefits. That's what 'conflict' theories try to do.

The 'conflict' picture of society

There's an alternative to seeing societies as harmonious wholes in which every part has a function. It's to see societies as areas of conflict, in which different groups struggle for dominance. On this view, the social structure at any one moment represents the balance of social forces, and inequality represents social domination, not social need.

There are many varieties of conflict theory, so different that for any other purpose they'd hardly deserve to be put into the same category. For instance, the theory that societies typically have a unified ruling class is deeply opposed to the theory that they commonly contain several competing elite groups with roughly equal power. But both are conflict theories. Conflict theories can also differ over how competing groups are identified, by concentrating on economic position or by using a variety of additional factors like sex, religion, nationality, or caste. But for our purposes these variations can be set to one side.

Conflict theories are very different from functionalism in the role they assign to inequality. Power, wealth, and prestige are seen as the stuff with which dominant groups reward *themselves*, and which they use to perpetuate their privileges. They use their position to foster a set of cultural values which promotes their own interests, not the interests of everyone. They take more or less as much as they can, limited only by what they have to bestow on the dominated to keep them at work and to fend off full-scale revolutions. But there is always potential opposition to their dominance. Changes brought into a society from abroad or born within the society itself can permit successful challenges from other groups, who can then cash in on their own new power.

Conflict and equality

On the face of it, conflict theories offer just as little hope for equality as functionalist views. They bring out the degree to which the rich and powerful have defended their privileges throughout history. And although they recognize that privileged groups can be challenged, they suggest that such challenges inevitably propel rising groups into their own positions of privilege. Dominant groups come and go, but dominance itself persists.

In spite of all this gloom, it's not hard to see why egalitarians have usually adopted a conflict picture of society. For one thing, that picture is at least honest about the causes of inequality, and doesn't dress up social power to look like Lady Bountiful. At the very least, it's better to see inequality as a powerful social evil than as something we should be grateful for.

But egalitarians also take a more positive approach. For suppose that power and privilege were attacked not by just another group on the make, but by an egalitarian movement. That would fit the general *pattern* of conflict theories – a successful egalitarian movement would establish its own outlook as dominant, and would use its power to consolidate and protect its own success. But in doing so it would be eliminating, as far as possible, inequality itself. Is this a realistic programme or a sociological fantasy?

Cynicism

A cynic might argue that a movement can look egalitarian without being so, and that this is just what a conflict view of society should lead us to expect. Any powerful movement will be hijacked by somebody for whom equality is no more than a useful slogan. Its leadership will amass power and will never give it up. In the 'equal' society which emerges, some will be 'more equal than others'.

Looking at the histories and structures of egalitarian movements, it's hard not to be cynical. 'Socialist' revolutions have installed new rulers but not many new equalities. Trade unions and socialist parties, though founded on equality, are often themselves sexist, racist, undemocratic, riddled with distinctions of status, and used for their leaders' own personal advancement. The situation in less formally structured areas like the women's movement is often not much better.

Cynicism is a convenient option if you're doing quite well already. It's not surprising that university professors, newspaper editors, and Tory politicians cast cynical slurs on egalitarian movements – they would, wouldn't they? It's different if you're a victim of inequality. Then, cynicism is only debilitating. Egalitarians should certainly be on guard against replacing old inequalities with new ones, but the cynic's taunt is in reality no more than a challenge to build genuinely egalitarian attitudes and practices.

Anyone can begin that process by examining their own motives and behaviour. If you can convince yourself that your own commitments are genuine, isn't it rather arrogant to doubt everyone else's? Are you so special, that only you can preserve your ideals in a sea of hypocrisy? The truth is that nearly all of us are capable of acting on a wide range of motives, from pure selfishness to complete idealism, and that we mostly act for a mixture of reasons. Progress towards equality depends on enough of us recognizing that it benefits ourselves as well as others, and being prepared to work together to promote it. That's not so hard to imagine.

But cynicism isn't the only attitude a conflict picture of society can engender. That picture reminds us of the power of dominant groups, and of their ability to use that power to prevent change. Maybe the right attitude to adopt towards the possibility of equality isn't cynicism, but pessimism.

Are the Enemies of Equality Too Strong?

Using a conflict picture of society makes you wonder about the conflict over *equality*, and about the relative power of the two sides. In particular, it makes you ask whether the opponents of equality operate from a position of insuperable strength – a strength which really does make equality impossible. But who are the enemies of equality, and what power do they have?

Conflict theories suggest that the opposition to equality is going to have two levels. The more basic level is the conflict of interests between equality and the privileged members of our society – the people who benefit most from existing inequalities. Since there are several principles of equality, there are several overlapping groups of people whose position equality threatens. Men in general benefit from sexual inequality, white people in general from racism, the rich from economic inequality, the powerful from political inequality. But there is a second level of conflict, that of beliefs and values. Some of the people who would lose their privileges as a result of equality nevertheless believe in it, while many of the people who would benefit are among its firmest opponents. Evaluating the prospects for equality would therefore involve looking at both kinds of conflict, for each of the principles of equality, and determining just how strong the opposition is. But we can get some idea of the scale of the problem by choosing an especially strong example. Most of the principles of equality have serious opponents, but among the strongest are the enemies of economic equality. So this section looks at them.

The opponents of economic equality

The central aims of economic equality are a much more equal division of income and wealth, democratic control of the economy, and decent, satisfying work for all. These aims conflict with the interests of the wealthy and economically powerful, among whom we might reasonably include anyone who'd lose at least half of their income, wealth, or power if complete equality were achieved. They're the ones with the most to protect. Who, then, are we talking about?

For income and wealth, it's a good approximation to include everyone who has more than double the average. For Britain, that's roughly the 10 per cent of all families who receive 23 per cent of income after taxes and transfers, and the 10 per cent of all families who own over half of all marketable wealth (basically wealth excluding pension rights). There is every reason to suppose that these two ten per cents are largely the same people: for instance, the top 10 per cent of income recipients get more than half of all investment income, over five times as much as the next 10 per cent.

For the US, greater inequality means that up to 20 per cent of the population, receiving 43 per cent of total income, can be counted among those with most to lose, corresponding to about 17 per cent of the population who own 75 per cent of all personal wealth. Again, it's reasonable to believe that these two groups largely coincide.

The calculation has to be different for economic power, since power is not only hard to quantify, but even hard to establish. For instance, it might be argued that the directors of small companies only have a little power, since their choices are so strongly limited by market forces. But this very objection suggests that we can get some idea of the scale of economic power by concentrating on the large, dominant companies in capitalist economies: those which, between them, account for at least half the economic activity in their field.

In Britain, the largest two hundred companies outside the financial sector control over half of the assets in their area. The financial sector is dominated by the 'big four' high street banks and a few large insurance companies and pension funds. Yet a recent study estimated that when you add up all the directors, top executives, and principal shareholders of the largest thousand companies, together with their families, you come up with between twenty-five and fifty thousand people, i.e. less than 0.1 per cent of the population. At a lower but still substantial level of economic power is the much larger number of people who *manage* companies. Managers as a group make up about ten to fifteen per cent of the working population.

The American economy is also very concentrated. One hundred manufacturing companies control over half of all manufacturing assets. Twenty transport, communications, and utility corporations control half of the assets in their sectors. Two thirds of banking and insurance assets are controlled by fifty banks and eighteen insurance companies. These 188 companies have about 3,500 presidents and directors between them, accounting for less than 0.01 per cent of the American population. Again, they are supported by a much larger number of managers.

There's no mystery about the relation between these holders of economic power and the top categories of income and wealth. The directors of large companies are paid high salaries and also own substantial investments. For instance, an American study on information covering 1940 to 1963 showed that the presidents of the largest fifty US industrials owned on average between one and two million dollars' worth of their companies' stocks. Another study of the five hundred largest US companies showed that half of their presidents owned at least half a million dollars worth of stock in their own firms. In Britain, a 1954 survey showed that company directors held more stock than any other elite or professional group: five times the averages for professional accountants and doctors.

Finally, we have to ask who has the strongest interest in stopping others from doing satisfying work. On the face of it, nobody. But Chapter 8 argues that unemployment is necessary for sustaining profits, and that job enrichment is restricted by the structure of capitalist enterprises. Capitalism also tends to use technology to replace skilled work, since unskilled labour is cheaper to hire and easier to control. The opponents of this aspect of economic equality are thus the groups we have already identified – the holders of wealth and economic power.

So if you want a general idea of who has the strongest interest in inequality, you can think of them as about a tenth of the population, with the particularly privileged group of large-scale capitalists at their core. They constitute the basic level of opposition to equality.

At the level of beliefs and values, things are more complicated. Undoubtedly some privileged people are personally rather well disposed towards equality, but they are certainly a minority. What's more worrying is that equality has fierce opponents in other ranks of society. If the arguments of this book are correct, their opposition is based on bad reasons – but it's still there. To understand it, we need to look at how the power of the privileged influences the beliefs of everyone else. Do they have the power to prevent equality?

The use of economic power

At the centre of the power of anti-egalitarians is *economic* power – power over the assets and activities of major capitalist companies. This power can be used most directly within these companies themselves: to maintain power structures, to determine pay and conditions, to allocate shares, and so on. But this internal power is obviously dependent on preserving the capitalist system, which seems open to a political challenge. How can that challenge be averted?

Most openly, the opponents of equality can defend their privileges against political attack by *using* economic power. Their primary weapon is control over investment. People used to worry about the 'brain drain', but the drain of capital is a much more serious threat. Modern international capitalism gives companies the choice of investing elsewhere if they don't like a government's policies. Closely allied to this form of economic power is the control exercised by the international banking system over the borrowing which every modern government relies on.

Economic power is also power over the information and skills which an egalitarian government would need to carry out its policies. If a British Labour government nationalized the top two hundred industrial companies under workers' control, who would they get to manage them? Of course, economic power also plays a traditional role in funding conservative parties and lobbyists.

But the open exercise of economic power needs to be reinforced by a widespread belief in inequality. How long, really, could the economically powerful withstand a determined commitment to equality on the part of a great majority of the population? It is therefore essential to prevent that commitment from developing. This is for the most part accomplished through the simple influence of daily habit. We are daily immersed in inegalitarian structures – they can seem like the only possibilities. And it's very hard to participate in the rat race without accepting its values, and coming to think of it as giving people what they deserve, or as promoting freedom, or as being the best system available. To a large extent, institutions like the mass media and the school system reinforce inequality in just this way, by reflecting the values of everyday life and acting as if there were no alternative.

Inequality can also win people's support through its influence on their sense of their own identity and of their own worth. It's not easy to spend your whole life thinking that you've been treated unjustly or that what you're doing is essentially a waste of time. Much better to find a way of accepting the system and your role within it. In doing so, you come to identify with how things are, however unequal – to take pride in such success as the system allows you, to take refuge in whatever forms of self-development the system makes available. Without any conscious effort, inequality has tamed you and weakened your potential for resistance.

Plainly the opponents of equality aren't satisfied with these passive influences, and so use other means to ensure that public opinion remains decidedly anti-egalitarian. Countries vary. In Britain, the main elements of this more overt influence on ideas are newspapers, schools, and the honours system. These institutions go out of their way to promote the message of inequality. The popular press is overwhelmingly attached to the Conservative Party, and constantly attacks socialism, feminism, trade unionism, and anything else that smacks of equality. The educational system grooms an elite in the public schools to be both holders of power and leaders of opinion. As of the early 1970s something like nine-tenths of top army officers, four-fifths of senior bishops, four-fifths of senior judges, two-thirds of top civil servants and three-quarters of all post-war Conservative MPs had a public school background. As for the honours system, it's enough to say that not only are the royal family and many hereditary peers among the very wealthiest families in the country, but of the life peerages created in this century a huge majority have been bestowed on the rich. The whole point of an honours system is to recognize merit. By concentrating its rewards on the rich and powerful, that system operates as a constant, explicit endorsement of Britain's economic structure.

The arguments for inequality are plausible enough on their own. They get reinforced day after day by the ordinary processes of living, by schools, by popular entertainment, by all the major newspapers, by the majority of VIPs, and by systems of public honour and recognition. Is it any wonder that people believe them?

Equality's weak friends

The opponents of equality seem well entrenched, and ready for anything you can throw at them. Compared to which the forces for equality often seem ill-equipped and badly organized. What are these weaknesses, and what can be done about them?

One problem is factionalism, and divisions on the political left are difficult to overcome. It might be put this way: there is only one existing world for anti-egalitarians to defend, but there are many possible worlds for egalitarians to aim for. Similarly, the tactics for defending the existing order are basically defensive – you simply oppose change. The tactics for changing the world involve imagination and choice, so there are bound to be disagreements over which tactics are right.

There is another deep source for the weakness of egalitarianism. A majority of people would benefit from equality. But each person has to decide whether throwing her or his energies into the struggle for equality is actually worth the candle. The more you stand to benefit from equality, the more likely it is that your current situation leaves you little time or energy, and that you feel too depressed to do anything in the first place. On the other hand, people with the time, energy, and organizational talent that egalitarianism needs may well prefer to pursue their own interests in an 'equal opportunity' society.

No matter who you are, you face what political theorists call the problem of collective action. Egalitarianism can only succeed by a collective effort to which your own individual contribution would be tiny. If enough other people get involved, it will succeed anyhow; if there aren't enough, your participation would be a waste of time. So either way, there's no point in getting involved. Of course, the same argument applies to virtually everyone. On that kind of reasoning, nobody will get involved and egalitarianism will fail.

A third weakness of egalitarian politics is that much of it suffers from the very inequalities it's supposed to be against. Many left-wing organizations lack democracy and a sense of community: many operate a status hierarchy based on position and personal connections. A glaring example is the predominance of white men in organizations like the Labour Party and most trade unions. It's not just that these inequalities contradict the principles such organizations are supposed to believe in. It's that in contradicting these principles, they rightly alienate many people who ought to be and want to be involved in egalitarian politics. But again, shortcomings of this kind are almost inevitable. How can we help but bring into egalitarian politics some of the inequalities most deeply ingrained in us by the society we live in?

None of these problems has a simple answer. Pious calls for unity and commitment are certainly not enough, especially when they come from people who want unity and commitment on their own terms. But we might reasonably hope for a little more tolerance. Not every tactical difference over the pursuit of equality counts as a betrayal.

It's also worth remembering the simple fact that the more satisfaction people get from their involvement in egalitarian politics, the more likely they are to participate in it. Just a sense of companionship and belonging can be satisfying. Other satisfactions could be generated by developing more meaningful forms of participation, of the sort described in Chapter 8. It might help to have more opportunities for sharing experiences in informal settings, and for cooperating on practical matters, like childcare and home repairs. Measures like that have a double benefit. They not only increase the enjoyment of

participating in egalitarian politics, but also make the participation itself more egalitarian.

All of these are issues for political practice. This discussion
is only meant to encourage the imagination and initiative they
certainly require.

The prospects for equality

Reflecting on even this sketchy account of the powers ranged
against equality and of its own weaknesses, how can an
egalitarian express any optimism? The most confident answer
is provided by a version of Marxism. Societies follow a pattern
of development, with feudalism leading to capitalism leading
to socialism. Capitalism brings about changes in itself, such as
large-scale production, increased productivity, an educated
workforce, and sophisticated planning techniques. These
create the social and economic conditions within which a
socialist transformation is not just possible but inevitable. By
possessing a theory of historical change, Marxism could
contrast its own view of the possibility of equality with the
'utopian' notions of people who dreamed of socialism but had
no idea of how to bring it about.

If something like this form of Marxism is true, then equality
has good prospects. If it is not true, then equality will depend
much more on factors which might go either way, like the
imagination and perseverance of egalitarians, the ability of
political leaders, and the impact of unforeseeable events. In
either case, it remains reasonable for egalitarians to retain
their hopes, and to work together for change. There have been
many power structures in the past which seemed invincible but
didn't last. The growth of the public sector of the economy,
although not on particularly egalitarian lines, has established a
base on which to build the skills and resources necessary to
challenge the power of capitalist firms. And movements of the
left have slowly and painfully gathered experience concerning
the powers ranged against them.

One thing is certain – equality will never come if we all
throw our hands up in despair. In the end, the strength of the
enemies of equality is not an argument against it, but a
challenge to its friends.

Local Versus Global Equality

The discussion of this chapter has followed the policy set out in Chapter 1 of concentrating on equality in one country. Yet unlike most of the other arguments in this book, it raises important problems about the relationship between equality in one country and equality world-wide. These problems move in two directions.

One direction is the impact of global inequality on any attempt to achieve greater equality in one place. The fact that modern capitalism is thoroughly international means that any capitalist country which tries to move dramatically towards equality faces confrontation with others, especially the US. Nobody has to guess whether this is true: it has been amply demonstrated in Chile and Nicaragua. There is a striking similarity to the problem faced by egalitarian movements in 'socialist' countries, where the main priority is more democracy. There, the threat of intervention is from the Soviet Union. The depressing irony is in how egalitarian movements within either sphere of influence can get driven into the arms of the other.

Foreign governments can act against equality not just through military support or invasion, as in Chile or Czechoslovakia, but also through economic support or sanctions. An obvious example is Cuba. There's the further problem, at least in the west, that both capital and skills will be attracted abroad. Of course you can try to restrict either of them from leaving the country, but that's difficult to achieve. In the case of emigration, it's also hard to justify. The freedom to leave is surely one of the basic rights egalitarians have strong reasons to support.

A better tactic in the long run is to concentrate on the other attractions your country has to offer its citizens, not the least of which might be its egalitarian atmosphere. But it's hard not to conclude that the best solution is for a great many countries to move towards equality more or less together. That doesn't mean that every country should wait until others have moved – who'd then move at all? It does mean that egalitarianism needs an internationalist dimension.

The importance of internationalism raises a second problem about the relation between national and global equality. For it would be unreasonable to expect poor countries to cooperate with the egalitarian movements of rich ones unless those movements were also committed to a global transfer of resources. Yet in terms of the argument earlier in this chapter, one might expect the populations of rich countries to oppose this transfer. Certainly, the evidence to date bears this out. A very simple example is the very low level of official development aid, currently about 0.36 per cent of the gross national products of OECD countries, and well under the 0.7 per cent cautiously recommended by the UN. When you remember that much of this 'aid' merely promotes the interests of multinationals, you begin to realize just how bad things are. In the international market, rich countries call the tune; poor countries cannot themselves force rich ones to give more aid or to improve the terms of trade.

So a pessimist could argue as follows. There will be no equality in any one country until there is global equality. But there will be no global equality because the rich countries will resist it and are powerful enough to block it. Therefore equality is impossible.

An optimist might reply that the situation is rather different. Greater equality does require both that a number of countries should move towards equality together and that there should be greater equality between rich countries and poor ones. But it is not beyond the capacity of egalitarian movements to pursue the two aims simultaneously. For example, developed countries with more egalitarian domestic policies also seem to have a better record on development aid and foreign trade: Norway, Denmark, Sweden, and the Netherlands all provide more than 0.7 per cent of their GNP in offical aid. More equality at home can create an awareness of the needs of others, too.

The uncertainties on both sides of this question are so immense that it really does seem more appropriate to call them pessimism and optimism than to treat them as solid arguments. But they do show that egalitarians cannot afford to think in purely national terms. One way or another, their aims will be affected by what happens elsewhere.

Are Anthropologists Reliable?

The main objections to the arguments of this chapter have to do with its use of anthropology, sociology, and statistics. Here are some examples.

It's all very well saying that the !Kung are egalitarian. But is it really legitimate to generalize from a single population in the Kalahari Desert?

The !Kung are not the only people reported to live in a broadly egalitarian way. Anthropologists have described a similar equality of circumstances in other foraging cultures, such as the Dogrib of the Canadian Northwest territories, the Copper Eskimos, some Australian Aborigines, the Paliyans of South India, the Guocyahi of Paraguay, the Mbuti in Africa. Descriptions of a high degree of sexual equality have included the G/Wi, Hadza, and Mbuti in Africa, the Agta in the Philippines, the Paliyans in India, and the Iroquois, Montagnais, Washo, and Wyandot Huron of North America.

These descriptions, like any piece of anthropology, may be false. But a non-anthropologist has to conclude on the basis of existing published evidence that broadly egalitarian societies have really existed, and therefore that equality is compatible with human nature.

But all those peoples are primitive. So equality may be possible, but only among primitive people.

One ought to be careful about using the term primitive. It suggests that these cultures are somehow not fully developed, not fully human. That's a piece of cultural superiority based on prejudice. But these cultures certainly have a very different technology, and involve living in fairly small groups.

So the examples do not prove that equality is possible in industrial societies. But that isn't their point. The point of the examples is to refute a particular claim: that inequality is part of human nature. For that, it's enough to find equality in any human society. You're then forced to explain why equality exists in some places but not in others. This chapter discusses the basic forms of such explanations.

In terms of that discussion, the argument that only primitive societies can be equal might be given in either a functionalist or a conflict form. The functionalist form would be to argue that an advanced technology and a large population require hierarchy. That sort of argument is considered above and found wanting. There is nothing to stop a large, technically advanced society from organizing itself democratically.

The conflict form of the argument might be something like this: that advanced technology and a large population provide the conditions under which one group can come to establish its dominance over others. That explanation of inequality has a lot to be said for it. But although it explains how inequality is possible, it doesn't prove that it's necessary. On the contrary, it suggests that technical advance may create the conditions for a challenge to inequality of the sort this chapter discusses.

In the end, the question of whether we can turn our own society into a more egalitarian one is wide open. Even if there had never been a broadly equal society, and even if equality had never been functional in the past, you still wouldn't know that equality is impossible. All you'd know is that its time had not yet come.

Why think that equality only threatens the interests of people with more than twice the average? Why not include everyone over the average?

The idea of using twice the average is based on three reasons. First of all, egalitarianism is not committed to completely equal incomes, for reasons of the sort discussed in Chapters 6 and 8. The very well off are thus more seriously threatened by equality than the moderately well off. In any case, the degree of economic inequality among people in the range below twice average income and wealth is less than it looks, since people's lifetime incomes are generally more equal than their incomes in any one year. Finally, it was argued in Chapter 8 that equality itself would bring many benefits concerning the character of one's work and control over one's life. These would compensate people who are moderately better off economically for what they'd lose from redistribution.

10

Miscellaneous Objections

This chapter takes up some of the remaining common objections to equality, objections which don't seem to fall under any general heading. Most of them are pretty thin, but that doesn't stop people making them. Here are some replies.

'Equality Would be Boring'

One of the most boring objections to equality is that equality would be boring. In its simplest form, it comes from assuming that equality means everyone being the same. But equality means no such thing. On the contrary, it means letting everyone develop their own capacities in a satisfying and fulfilling way.

A more highbrow complaint is that an egalitarian society would stifle genius and creativity in a morass of mass culture. But why should it? Because there would be no artists dying from consumption in Parisian garrets? Well, perhaps not – but even if a certain kind of creativity does come out of pain and anguish, there is no risk that an egalitarian society would abolish them. No one seriously believes that equality means the end of illness and death, of emotional trauma, of frustrated ambitions, of guilt and remorse, or of countless other sorrows. Do artists really need poverty and degradation as well?

The argument that creativity would suffer from a lack of rich benefactors is equally groundless. Undoubtedly an egalitarian society would have to finance the arts in ways different from our own, and a sensible policy would have to provide for the well-known fact that judgments of artistic ability and value vary enormously. It would therefore make sense, for instance, to provide for many independent centres of decision-making, so that nobody had a monopoly over who was encouraged and who struggled away on their own resources. It's a difficult business, and public funding for the arts is bound to produce greater controversy than a system in which rich people use 'their own' money to keep artists going. But no one can pretend that private patronage has on the whole been any better – that it hasn't been squandered on conformity and mediocrity as much as public money ever has. In both cases, it's a question of a portion of society's resources being used to support a certain range of activities: the resources aren't any the less wasted if wasted by private individuals rather than public authorities.

Would Equality Make any Difference?

It's widely believed that equality would have little impact on the people it's supposed to benefit. That belief is false.

In the case of incomes, just consider some figures. In Britain, the poorest ten per cent of the population, five and a half million people, receive about three per cent of total income after tax and transfers. Under strict equality of income, they would get ten per cent of the total, more than three times what they're getting now – obviously a substantial increase! Even a mildly egalitarian programme in which no one received less than half the average income would give the worst-off ten per cent of the population at least five per cent of the total – an increase of two-thirds or more.

In the US, the poorest twenty per cent receive about four per cent of total income. Under strict equality, their income would multiply by five to twenty per cent of the total. On the 'mild' principle, it would still be two and a half times what they get now.

A redistribution of wealth would be even more dramatic, since some people have literally no wealth at all. In Britain eighty per cent of the population together own only twenty-three per cent of marketable wealth; in the US the figures are much the same. So again, even on a mildly egalitarian principle of nobody having less than half or more than twice average wealth, the average wealth of three quarters of the population would more than double, and the wealth of the worst off would increase immensely.

But talking about the distribution of wealth in these financial terms can be misleading, since wealth is more a question of control over resources than of money in the bank. An egalitarian programme of economic democracy would give people much more control over resources than a simple redistribution of the wealth now in private hands, but might not involve a big increase in their own privately held marketable property. For instance, co-ops are normally based on the principle that even though the business is jointly owned, no one can sell her or his share. The general point here, discussed at length in Chapter 7, is that the property system of an egalitarian society could be so different from our own that simple comparisons of property ownership might not make much sense. What *would* make sense is a comparison in terms of the power people exercise over their own lives.

This redistribution of economic power, and the other changes brought about by greater democracy, make for a less measurable effect of equality, but an important one. And a greater equality of respect would also have a valued impact on people's lives. The idea that equality wouldn't really change things is utterly mistaken.

One more misconception worth correcting is the idea that equality doesn't matter because everyone gets better off over time. If real incomes, i.e. incomes relative to inflation, double every few years anyway, what's so important about equality? The answer to the objection has three parts. First of all, it's simply not true that the real income of the poor is constantly rising. In Britain, government policy has typically been to increase pensions and benefits – the main income of the poor – only in line with inflation, making for no real increase at all.

Secondly, an increase in real income may not be a real improvement in satisfying needs. That depends not only on whether the statistical index used for defining 'inflation' is geared to the needs of the poor, but also on whether increases in real incomes are accompanied by the development of new needs, in the way described in Chapter 2.

Thirdly, the objection assumes that indefinite economic growth is both possible and desirable. But it may well be neither. Given the earth's limited resources, the effect of mass marketing on people's lives and values, and the tendency of economic growth to create new needs which swallow up increased production, there are strong reasons for doubting the wisdom of an indefinite commitment to growth. Nothing in the egalitarian view of things implies such a commitment, given an appropriate conception of what people need.

All these points accept the objection's concentration on the question of income. But, again, income is only one of equality's concerns. A rising real income doesn't necessarily give people any more power or a higher status or more satisfying work. Even if the objection were a valid argument against income equality, it wouldn't show that those other equalities didn't matter.

'The Politics of Envy'

When egalitarianism is called the 'politics of envy', or said to express class hatred or resentment, its critics are using what logicians call an 'ad hominem' argument: an argument 'against the person', not against the belief. As with all ad hominem arguments, it has an easy answer. For the question of whether a belief is justified is quite independent of the personal motives which might make people want to believe it. The arguments for equality don't disappear just because some of the people who accept them are envious or resentful. By the same token, the arguments for inequality are distinct from the smug complacency of some of the people who believe in them.

But is the 'politics of envy' line even a fair complaint against the people who believe in equality? Do their attitudes towards the rich and powerful really demand an apology? Or do they feel justified anger, justified resentment, and justified antipathy, which the charge of envy attempts to devalue and weaken?

The managing director of a British company was paid three quarters of a million pounds in 1984, at a time when a family of four would have been lucky to get £70 a week in welfare payments. There's nothing wrong in being angry about that, in resenting his privileged position, or in feeling that, however nice a person he might be to have a quiet chat with, you would also feel a certain antagonism towards him – because of his position, because of what he stands for. These are perfectly legitimate reactions, each in its way based on the reasonable belief that this man both represents and actively perpetuates an unjust social system. Nobody would question these reactions if we were talking about attitudes towards some police-state dictator or gangster. But in all of these cases, the emotions involved are justified by the beliefs underlying them.

When people describe all that anger, resentment, and dislike as mere envy, they are in effect *denying* those underlying beliefs. They're saying that the supposed justifications are really rationalizations for a groundless rancour at the good fortune of others. The message is that nothing's really wrong, that nobody's really to blame, and that the solution is for egalitarians to go off and sort out their feelings. The 'politics of envy' charge is thus much more closely related to arguments for and against equality than it seems, for it only makes sense on the assumption that the case for equality is inadequate. Egalitarians should respond to it not by shrinking away defensively, but by pointing out that there is quite a different explanation for their feelings towards the privileged – namely, that the case for equality is compelling.

All this is not to deny that people sometimes do envy the privileged. You could hardly expect otherwise in a culture which not only tolerates but practically worships wealth and power, and which pretends that they are signs of personal worth. Envy is certainly distasteful and destructive; it would be altogether better if egalitarians were free of it. But given that the culture of inequality nurtures envy, isn't it a little unfair to complain that egalitarianism feeds on it? Yet equality can never be reduced to envy: not unless every argument in its favour is illusory.

'Middle Class' Socialists

The critics of equality seem to have an easy target when it comes to 'middle class' socialists. If these self-styled egalitarians really believed what they say, why don't they give away their money? Why do they live in fashionable neighbourhoods? Why don't they send their children to inner-city schools?

Logically speaking, these attacks are irrelevant to the truth of egalitarianism. Like the 'politics of envy' argument, they are ad hominem, against the person. And so the same easy answer is available here: that even if some egalitarians were hypocrites, the case for equality wouldn't evaporate. But the argument seems to have a certain persuasive power. Why should anyone believe in equality when some of its most vocal defenders obviously don't? It seems to show that equality isn't supposed to be taken seriously, that it's a pious wish that salves the consciences of the privileged. Equality is for saying, not doing – just another slogan for another political game.

In some forms, the criticism is completely groundless. If all someone means by 'middle class' is having a white collar job or a university degree or a certain way of talking or dressing, then the idea that there's some contradiction between being middle class and being an egalitarian is simply mistaken. For none of these show anything about what a person believes or values, and so they show nothing that can even begin to feature in a contradiction.

The real problem arises when people who claim to be egalitarians are at the same time enjoying a privileged life. Doesn't that contradict their view that *nobody* should be privileged?

An initial defence against the objection is that it misunderstands what egalitarians stand for. Equality doesn't mean equal misery: it means that everyone should enjoy many of the benefits now possessed by a minority. Everyone should have a challenging education, should live in a decent neighbourhood, should have satisfying work. How could it possibly promote equality in this sense for middle class egalitarians to give these things up? That wouldn't be a step towards equality at all.

A defence along those lines has a lot to be said for it when it's about things which really could be enjoyed by everyone, like good education and good housing. But it starts to sound hollow when the benefits in question are by their very nature comparative. Private schooling, for instance, is not just 'good education' if it's intended to give its pupils advantages over other children. Similarly, the point of private health care, at least in Britain, is to get better service than other people with the same needs. The point is even clearer with other kinds of inequality, such as exercising undemocratic power, accepting and using undeserved prestige, engaging in or profiting from racism, sexism, or exploitation. Egalitarians are supposed to want these things abolished, not universalized.

Any egalitarian hoping to defend those sorts of privilege has to go beyond the argument for universal benefits. The most plausible strategy is to argue that there's a distinction between the kind of society a person believes in and the choices it's reasonable to make in our own society. For instance, you can believe that a good society would be completely non-violent without thinking that you shouldn't defend yourself against a violent attack. Similarly, believing in an equal society doesn't make it unreasonable to accept advantages in an unequal one. In an inegalitarian society, even well-off people feel vulnerable for themselves and their children. Our society makes it difficult to think that you ever have enough, when you always feel you have to keep on running just to stay in the same place. For imagine you gave away a fortune, and the next day found yourself disabled and out of work – that's the kind of thought that makes middle class egalitarians hang on to what they've got.

Understandable as it is, this line of reasoning isn't entirely convincing. For the central arguments in favour of an equal society are also arguments for refusing privileges in an unequal one. If people's basic needs are in general more important than luxuries, then the basic needs of destitute people today are more important than your luxuries. If it's wrong in general to exploit and degrade people, then it's wrong today for you to exploit and degrade them. If undemocratic power restricts people's freedom in general, then your use of it today is a restriction. Of course rejecting privilege has its risks – but it also has its costs. The distinction between principles for the future and principles for the present may work in some areas, but it's often flimsy.

It seems more honest to admit that people who profess egalitarian beliefs but live privileged lives are compromising between their moral values and their self-interest. That's a compromise which nearly everyone makes in some way or other, and by its very nature not open to a reasoned defence – since reason alone will simply tell you not to compromise in the first place. Perhaps the only argument still available is against people who are very critical of such compromises: do they really avoid them in their own lives? But that's an ad hominem argument, too.

The fact that some egalitarians are prepared to compromise their beliefs is not an argument against egalitarianism itself. It does not prove that an egalitarian society is impossible because, as argued in Chapters 8 and 9, equality and self-interest would operate hand in hand in an equal society. Nor does it prove that we can never make an equal society out of our own, since for the majority of people the compromise does not even arise. What it does show is that the most privileged sections of society are the most likely to resist equality in spite of its moral appeal – an issue also discussed in Chapter 9.

Philosophical Method

The approach of this book is to argue for the principles of equality on the basis of widely held moral values. The central arguments are that these values either imply egalitarianism or are at least compatible with it. In each case, the argument goes as far as is necessary to sustain a certain implication or compatibility, and no further. Any attempt to provide some 'deeper' justification for equality has been deliberately avoided.

People with a philosophical training or inclination may find such an approach unsatisfying. They may want to know the grounds for the widely held values which the arguments employ, and the grounds for those grounds, pursuing the question to some ultimate 'foundation'. Only then, they might argue, has equality really been defended. Part of their dissatisfaction may also stem from the necessarily pluralistic character of the argument of this book – the fact that it begins and ends with a *number* of values and principles, and that the several arguments have a certain independence from each other. There are two main reasons why I have not tried to satisfy these longings for a unitary, foundational approach.

First of all there is a practical reason. In practice, political argument does start from the values and principles people already believe in. Each step away from these beliefs increases potential resistance. So practically speaking, arguments will be more effective if they preserve as much as possible of people's initial beliefs. Arguments which go beyond these beliefs to their speculative grounds are at best spare wheels; at worst, they set up unnecessary targets.

But there's also a philosophical reason. It's that the picture of moral reasoning which creates these longings for foundations and unity is in my view deeply mistaken. The wish to construct a moral system from absolutely certain fundamental assumptions is based on a misunderstanding – essentially, on thinking that the everyday activity of giving reasons for beliefs must lead back to some reason which does not itself need and could not be given any further justification. It's like people thinking that since tables rested on floors, and floors on the earth, the earth had to rest on something else – but what did *that* rest on?

If moral thinking is not conceived of as stretching back to some fundamental source, then the idea that it may involve several relatively independent concerns might not seem so implausible. Even if morality did have a 'foundation', that might still be a foundation for a plurality of values rather than a single one. In the end, the choice between a unitary and a pluralistic picture of moral values is sustained by seeing that any attempt to force all values into a single mould only distorts them and blunts our moral sensitivity.

I hope that these brief remarks help to explain how philosophical issues have affected the precise nature of this book. For anyone who takes a different view, the book may seem incomplete, and some of its arguments unnecessary. But on any philosophical view, most of the arguments addressed here will come to the surface sooner or later. They are to that degree independent of any particular account of the nature of moral judgment.

Some Conclusions

This chapter looks back over the rest of the book by briefly summarizing its arguments; it then discusses some practical issues concerning the politics of equality. What should egalitarians have as their priorities? How should they relate to other political trends? What should they actually be doing?

A Brief Summary of the Arguments

Part One discusses the meaning and basic grounds of equality. Equality is defined in Chapter 1 as a group of principles: the satisfaction of basic needs, respect for others as equals, economic equality, political equality, and racial, sexual, ethnic and religious equality. As the central issue in this book is to defend these principles, questions about the organization of an egalitarian society are largely secondary. But Chapter 1 says a little about the relationships between equality, socialism, democracy, and the welfare state – themes which arise again in later chapters.

The main grounds for equality come from thinking about human needs, mutual respect, and a sense of community. Chapter 2 shows how the principle of satisfying basic needs follows from concern for human welfare, and how that concern implies a more general commitment to the principles of equality. The varieties of respect for others reviewed in Chapter 3 supply further arguments for the principles of equality, since inequalities are usually unfair, degrading, exploitative, or elitist. Chapter 4 shows the ways in which a sense of community both fosters and is encouraged by greater equality. Anyone who has a serious concern for the wellbeing of others, who is committed to treating others decently, and who values a sense of community has strong reasons to believe in equality. Together, these are the three basic grounds on which egalitarianism rests.

With other values, the argument is not so clear: they are often alleged to be on the side of inequality. Part Two examines these allegations in detail. Chapter 5 considers the first issue – whether equality should be confined to the idea of 'equality of opportunity'. It shows how everything that matters about equality of opportunity points to the much more extensive equality of egalitarianism. The following chapter explodes the idea that the privileged deserve their position, either as a reward for excellence or a compensation for their trouble. An egalitarian society would actually incorporate some kinds of desert, but would keep its inegalitarian tendencies under control.

The fear that equality would destroy freedom is addressed in Chapter 7. The only freedom threatened by equality is the freedom of the rich and powerful to use their privileges for their own advantage: equality would actually increase the freedom of everybody else. In particular, equality involves a strong commitment to individual development and to democratic rights. Nor, as Chapter 8 shows, is substantial inequality beneficial for society as a whole. It's not necessary for motivating people, for avoiding bureaucratic waste, or for ensuring competent decisions. In fact, equality offers a wide range of benefits which inequality rules out.

But is equality possible? Chapter 9 shows that nobody has proven otherwise. Natural differences between people don't have to lead to social inequality; inequality isn't needed for social survival. The only obstacle to the possibility of equality is the power of its opponents – but they aren't necessarily invincible. Finally, Chapter 10 shows how weak some remaining objections to equality really are. Equality wouldn't destroy our culture. It would make a real difference to people's lives. And it can't be dismissed as the 'politics of envy' or by attacking 'middle class socialists' – those are just cheap jibes.

The arguments of this book show that the most common

objections to egalitarianism are unfounded. On the contrary, they show that the values commonly used to attack equality actually support it. They also emphasize some of the key features of an egalitarian outlook. Egalitarianism, like any other serious political perspective, is a complicated set of beliefs. It doesn't stand for everyone being the same, but for every individual's needs and capacities being catered for. It stands for a society in which people are respected for their personal qualities, not their social position – a society in which inequalities of income balance out inequalities of need and work, instead of reinforcing them. It stands for a democratic society, not a bureaucratic one. And it stands for a society in which genuine differences of sex, religion, and culture are respected, not despised. These principles of equality need and reinforce each other. Inequalities of wealth restrict democracy and mutual respect. Inequalities of power sustain economic advantage and social prestige. Inequalities of status imply that the rich and powerful deserve their privileges. Egalitarianism is a complex set of beliefs, but the beliefs hang together.

There are doubtless other arguments for and against equality, certainly other nuances and variations. But the arguments in this book show that the case for equality is formidable, and often indicate ways in which other anti-egalitarian arguments are likely to fail. What does that mean in practice?

What Should Egalitarians Do?

Getting from the realm of argument to that of practice raises some difficult issues. Although some of these are addressed in the course of arguing for equality, there are three major tasks which ought to be touched on: establishing priorities, relating to movements which aren't explicitly egalitarian, and deciding how to engage in the politics of equality itself. All three of these questions go beyond the main concerns of this book: my point is only to raise them.

Equalities in order of priority

Equality is not an all or nothing affair. Many countries have already achieved equalities such as universal suffrage, freedom from slavery, and the satisfaction of subsistence needs:

equalities which were once thought inconceivable. Other equalities still look like distant aims. It makes sense for egalitarians to think realistically about their priorities, to build on existing equalities, and to be guided by both moral urgency and political practicality.

The defence and extension of provisions for satisfying people's most urgent needs are obvious priorities, as are the defence and extension of basic rights against slavery, torture and political imprisonment. The immediate political agenda clearly includes advances against racism and sexism, particularly in jobs, education and politics. More democracy at work, more participation in local affairs, and more public control over economic power are certainly three aims for which egalitarians should be drawing up detailed programmes. And since equalities are interdependent, such programmes have to be intertwined.

There is always the danger in declaring priorities that lower priorities will simply be forgotten. But one of the recurring ideas of this book is that many egalitarian aims depend on the growth of a popular commitment to equality. It follows that egalitarians should never allow current priorities to stifle the open discussion and endorsement of longer-term goals. Otherwise those will never be achieved at all.

Equality and other movements

Some of the central political issues of our time are only indirectly connected with equality. That is no reason for egalitarians to ignore them. There is the whole area of 'green' politics: protecting the environment, questioning the need for heavy industry and nuclear power, producing real, uncontaminated food. There is the peace movement. And there is the women's movement: much of it directly concerned with equality, but extending to many other areas, including the exploration of different ideals of human wellbeing.

It's not difficult to see connections between these and equality. They can be seen, for instance, in those interweaving strands of the women's movement. Nuclear weapons can be understood as the ultimate expression of male dominance and as the inevitable result of an industrial economy built on a sexual division of labour. It can also be argued that the insights which lie behind the demands for sexual equality also support a shift of personal values, in which both the 'masculine' and the 'feminine' have a place in everyone's life.

Other forms of the connection could be described; I don't wish to deny them. But they are distant enough and controversial enough to take them beyond any basic defence of egalitarianism. The rest of this book makes it clear, I hope, that there is no essential conflict between equality and either peace or ecology or feminist values. How strongly they reinforce each other is a question I leave open.

The politics of equality

Equality doesn't develop by accident. It results from the conscious efforts of political movements opposed to power and privilege. Anyone who takes equality seriously has to take seriously a commitment to egalitarian politics. By definition, that politics has to oppose racism and sexism. If the arguments of this book are sound, then it must also be socialist in the broad sense of promoting a democratically planned economy. Socialist politics takes many forms: the choice between them is not at issue here. What matters is seeing that equality without politics is impossible.

The politics of equality needs to be based on strong principles, but it needs detailed programmes as well. This book has concentrated on general arguments, bringing in institutional questions only when necessary. Those questions – about economic planning, worker management, the role of the state, forms of democracy, education, family life, broadcasting, religion, health care, transportation, and so on – are already being addressed with imagination and skill by many egalitarians. Some of the most interesting new ideas have come not from self-styled 'experts' but from workplace, neighbourhood, and consumer groups trying to shape their own futures. Their efforts need to be encouraged, publicized, and emulated on a much wider scale.

But equality is not an end in itself: it only matters because of its effect on people's lives. And a life dedicated to political activity isn't everybody's idea of fulfilment! Nobody has a duty to devote their whole life to politics, and yet there's also no such thing as an apolitical life. For how we relate to each other in 'private' either supports or challenges the way power and privilege are structured in society as a whole. To put it another way, equality is concerned not just with the structure of whole societies, but with human relationships in general. No one person can change the whole world. But each of us can make a start – if only by arguing for equality.

Glossary

Generally, these are technical terms or ordinary terms which I use with a special sense.

argument   In everyday speech, an *argument* is a disagreement or quarrel. I use 'argument' in its other sense, to mean a reasoned defence for some belief.

benefit-all argument   An argument for inequality of the following form: Everyone would be better off if such-and-such an inequality existed than they would be if people were equal in this respect; therefore the inequality is a good thing. These arguments are related to what economists sometimes mean by *efficiency*, but as a rather special case.

bureaucracy, bureaucratic   I use *bureaucracy* in the broad sense to mean a large, formally structured organization, such as is found in both private companies and state institutions. I follow everyday use in calling these organizations *bureaucratic* when their internal rules and regulations seem to interfere with achieving their supposed aims.

capital, capitalist   I use *capital* in accordance with popular usage to mean the means of production in a *market economy*, in which these means are privately owned by a minority of the population and thus in which the majority of people have no access to the means of production except by selling their *labour*. Such an economy is a *capitalist* economy, and I loosely refer to the owners and controllers of capital as *capitalists*.

Actually, popular usage is a little inconsistent. Marx says that capital can be thought of either in terms of the money necessary to engage in production, or in terms of the factors of production which the money is used to buy. These include both 'fixed capital' (raw materials, machines, buildings, and so on), which he calls the means of production, and 'variable capital' (the *labour power* of employees). Popular usage sometimes agrees with Marx, but sometimes limits itself to fixed capital. In this book, these distinctions don't play any role, so you can think of capital either way.

class In ordinary usage, *class* is variously defined in terms of income, wealth, occupation, life style, and family background. Marxists and other social theorists use more exact categories. For the purpose of this book, ordinary usage is sufficient, since it emphasizes the way in which our society links inequalities of work situation with those of wealth, *income*, *power*, and *status*, and how it passes these inequalities along from one generation to the next.

compatible, incompatible Two statements or beliefs are *compatible* if it is possible for both to be true. They are *incompatible* if it is not possible for both to be true.

concept See *idea*

consistent, inconsistent Two statements or beliefs are *consistent* if they are *compatible*; they are *inconsistent* if they are *incompatible*. One statement or belief is inconsistent if it contains two inconsistent parts; otherwise it is consistent.

contradict, contradiction One statement *contradicts* another if they cannot both be true. A *contradiction* is the assertion of two contradicting statements at once.

democratic, democracy, participatory democracy A power structure is *democratic* to the extent that the people it governs have equal *power* over its decisions. Whether this is best accomplished by majority rule is an open question – often it is, sometimes it's not. A system which does a reasonably good job at sharing power equally is a *democracy*. Since this requires much more popular participation in the decision making process than we're used to, I sometimes emphasize this point by talking of *participatory democracy*.

desert, deserve *Desert* is the noun-form of *deserve*. It is pronounced with the accent on the second syllable, as in the phrase 'just deserts'. I distinguish two special kinds of desert.

Merit desert applies when you are said to deserve something in virtue of some prior evaluation of your characteristics or actions. Compensation desert applies when you are said to deserve to be compensated for some loss, harm, or deficiency.

distributive justice   See *justice*

efficiency   In general, *efficiency* is effectiveness in achieving given ends. When I discuss the issue of *bureaucratic* inefficiency, I am using this everyday meaning.

Two more specific senses used by economists are sometimes called 'productive' and 'allocative' efficiency. In the first sense, one productive process is more efficient than another if it produces more output for the same input; but note that on this definition you can only compare processes for efficiency when you can compare inputs and outputs, for instance by reducing everything to money value. That's not much use when you're discussing the merits of different social institutions in which money prices wouldn't be constant.

In the second sense, one allocation of goods is more efficient than another if at least one person prefers the first to the second, and nobody prefers the second to the first. (Instead of 'prefers', you might say 'is better off under'.) Note that on this definition also it is often impossible to compare allocations: if you prefer one and I prefer the other, neither is more efficient. This is likely to be the case for any two social institutions which allocate goods in very different ways.

Because in general the value of efficiency depends on the aims in question, and because the specific senses used by economists are for the most part just not applicable to the big questions about equality versus inequality, it's important not to get carried away by the slogan of 'efficiency versus equality'. But in Chapter 8 I've tried to discuss the issues which the contrast between efficiency and equality usually raises.

egalitarian, equalitarian   I use *egalitarian* to mean a person who believes in equality, and particularly one who believes in the principles of equality set out in Chapter 1. I also use it as an adjective to mean 'of or pertaining to the beliefs of egalitarians'. Some people use the term *equalitarian* instead; it isn't as easy on the ear.

equity   Used in everyday speech with the same looseness as *fairness*, I have tried not to use it at all.

fair, fairness These are rather general *moral* terms connected with *justice*, particularly related to the ideas of impartiality in judgment and open competition. In some contexts, fair is synonymous with equal, while in others it can be as general as 'reasonable'. Being such a loose and flexible idea, it seems wise not to place too much weight on it.

follows One statement or belief *follows* from another if the other *implies* it.

functional, functionalism In a *functional* explanation, an event or situation is explained by indicating its function: that is, its role in bringing about certain effects. For instance, it is a functional explanation of why bicycles have gears to say that gears make it easier to ride uphill, and it is a functional explanation of poverty to say that poverty is necessary for profits.

By *functionalism*, I mean the particular sociological approach which explains things in terms of their value to society. In fact, this is only one version of what social theorists might call functionalism.

ground A *ground* for a belief is a reason for holding it.

idea, concept I use these terms fairly colloquially. An *idea* can be a belief; it can also be what one understands by a certain word or expression, such as the idea of equality. The second of these senses is also covered by the term *concept*.

implies, implication To say that one statement *implies* another means that if the first statement is true, then the second is also true. Hence the *implications* of a statement are those other statements which are true if the original statement is true.

income In everyday conversation, *income* means the amount of money a person receives in a given time period. It is more accurate, however, to think of money income in terms of the set of bundles of goods and services that money can buy at existing prices, and to think of total income as this income plus income in kind (e.g. employment perks and publicly provided goods and services). But this more accurate conception makes comparisons between different incomes more difficult: in two different economies, the same goods may not be available, may be sold at different prices, or may be provided in different ways. In particular, money income ratios in different countries may be quite misleading if they involve different levels of public provision and subsidy.

In accepting the idea of some people earning 'twice as much as average', I am talking about post-tax money incomes and assuming for the sake of argument that levels of public provision and of purchasing power are similar to those found in contemporary industrial capitalist economies. Naturally, things would be rather different in a socialist economy and figures would have to be justified accordingly.

individualism, individuality The problem with *individualism* is that it means too many things. It can mean that individuals should put their own interests ahead of other people's, in contrast to the idea of altruism. Or it can mean that individuals should have to provide for their own needs, in contrast to the idea of collective provision. It can mean simply that individuals are important, in contrast to an ethic which values only groups. And it can mean other things, too: see the book by Lukes listed in 'References and Further Reading'. So I've tried not to use it except where nothing else will do.

The idea of *individuality* is less of a problem. A person's individuality consists of her or his particular character, tastes, and capacities. In this book, I accept the widely held belief that the freedom of individuals to develop their individuality is important. I argue that an egalitarian society would promote this freedom.

justice, distributive justice, social justice Although these terms (or at least two of them) figure frequently in ordinary political discussion, there is a lot of controversy over them in philosophy. For instance, some authors insist that *justice* is concerned only with *rights*; and since some of the aims of egalitarians might be better described as social ideals rather than as anything anyone has a right to, this view would deny that egalitarianism is a belief about justice. The term *distributive justice* is more specific, and generally used to refer to the kinds of question discussed in this book. But it has a tendency to be a little narrower than that, for instance to concern only the distribution of *income*, which excludes many of the issues talked about here. The same problem arises with the term *social justice*; besides which, nowadays 'social justice' is often taken in political discussion to mean a particular view about society, namely an egalitarian one. So this book could be taken to be a defence of something which goes beyond justice, or of one opinion about justice, or of social justice itself! It seems more constructive to try not to rely too much on these terms at all. But you are perfectly welcome to translate the arguments into arguments about social justice if you think it would help.

labour, labour power It is natural to think that in a *capitalist* economy workers sell their *labour* to their employers, and that's how I've expressed myself here. But there is an interesting argument in Marx for thinking of workers as selling their *labour power*, that is, their capacity to work. Nothing much hangs on that here, but I wouldn't want to be seen as taking sides on it.

market, market economy People use *markets* to buy and sell goods and services; a market allocates goods and services by exchange. But markets can operate according to different ground-rules, defined by different systems of *property rights*. In a *market economy*, markets are the dominant means for allocating goods and services, including of course the means of production. Most market economies are *capitalist*, but it is possible to have a market economy in which the means of production are socially owned, for instance by workers' cooperatives. Market economies may of course involve a certain amount of economic *planning* (for instance, within firms and in deciding the rules by which markets will operate), but this is seen as secondary to and facilitating the operation of markets themselves.

market socialism See *socialism*

meritocracy Literally, rule by those with merit; but the use of this word usually implies that merit is being thought of in terms of formal qualifications and certified ability.

moral, morality Sometimes ordinary usage thinks of *morality* only in connection with special areas, like sexual morality. But I use the term to mean the whole area of consideration of what's right and wrong. In this sense, egalitarianism is a moral question, and moral *argument* is necessary to resolve it.

override When two *values* or *principles* conflict, the one which is stronger is said to *override* the other.

participatory See *democratic*

philosophy In everyday use, a person's *philosophy* is her or his outlook on life, and in this sense egalitarianism is at least part of a personal philosophy. But since academic philosophy has rather different and more specialized concerns, I try to avoid confusion by restricting my use of the term to discussions of those special types.

planning, planned economy Economic *planning* is the conscious coordination of economic activities. All real economies involve some planning, but I use the term *planned economy* for an economy in which the allocation of goods and services is dominated by decisions taken for the whole economy by some central authority; inevitably, that means that this authority will control major decisions of investment, production, and the distribution of income. Where the authority is *democratic* in structure and the means of production are socially owned, the economy is *socialist*. Planned economies may use *markets* in some areas, but the rules by which such markets operate will themselves be consciously planned, and the scope of markets will be limited.

political I use *political* in the broad sense to talk about the distribution of *power* throughout a society, and not just about government. I also occasionally use it in the even broader sense to talk about any issue affecting the general arrangements of life in society. In this sense, egalitarianism is a question of politics, even when not directly concerned with questions of power.

power I use *power* in the everyday sense of the ability to act or to achieve one's aims, especially but not necessarily by having control over others.

premise In an *argument*, the *premises* are the statements from which the conclusion is supposed to *follow*.

principle A statement of what ought to be done, or ought to be the case.

property See *rights*

racism, race For the purposes of this book, *racism* can be understood as the attitudes and institutions which systematically favour people with one skin-colour over people with another – in our society, white people over black people. Since the term *race* is used by racists to imply a general association of skin colour with other characteristics, I have tried to avoid using it myself. I use the expression 'racial equality' to mean a commitment to a society in which no colour-group is systematically favoured over any other.

rights, property rights Roughly speaking, a person has a *right* to something if others have an obligation to provide it or not to take it away. If the obligation in question is a *moral* obligation, we can talk about a moral right; if a legal obligation, a legal right.

Obviously, legal rights exist only as a result of certain institutional arrangements (namely, laws passed by established governments). The same kind of thing is true of some moral rights, too: for instance, the moral right you acquire when someone promises to do something for you only exists because of the social institution of promise-making.

Property rights are rights over the use of 'objects' taken in the broadest sense to include, e.g., songs, inventions, computer programs. I leave open the question of whether property rights are moral rights or only legal rights, but I argue in Chapter 7 that in either case they depend on changeable institutional arrangements.

social justice See *justice*

social structure Any way of organizing relationships within a society or social group.

socialism, market socialism I use *socialism* to mean a *democratic*ally *planned economy* in which the means of production are under social ownership. Since this definition excludes countries like the USSR, China and Cuba, because of their limited democracy, I usually call them 'socialist' in quotation marks. This is not meant to detract from what these countries have achieved by planning their economies, but does express their distance from the socialist ideal. I mean social ownership to have a broad sense so that it has many forms, including both state ownership and at least certain kinds of cooperative.

Market socialism, as the name implies, gives *markets* or their equivalent an important role, but subject to social ownership and overall planning.

status Although it has many possible meanings, I use *status* in what seems the commonest usage, to mean a person's position in a socially determined hierarchy of honour or prestige, signifying social superiority and inferiority. As Weber points out, status may or may not go along with economic position, but there is at least an indirect connection because status is usually expressed in a life style which has to be paid for and is usually determined by a person's occupation. In everyday usage, though, these aspects of status are usually called *class*.

term Word.

theory A *theory* attempts to unify and structure an area of knowledge. The main theories discussed in this book try either to explain social or economic facts, or to justify moral and political *principles*.

they, their, them I have freely used *they*, *their* and *them* as singular pronouns in constructions following 'everyone', 'anyone', etc., as in 'giving everyone real influence over the decisions which affect them.' For a justification, see Miller and Swift in 'References and Further Reading'.

utilitarianism The *theory* that the rightness and wrongness of actions, policies, institutions, etc. are determined by adding together all their costs and benefits without taking any account of how these costs and benefits are distributed. Historically, utilitarians judged costs and benefits in terms of 'happiness', itself defined in terms of pleasure and pain. Other versions of utilitarianism can be constructed using other conceptions of *wellbeing*.

values, value judgments A person's *values* are the standards she or he uses to judge the importance, goodness, or desirability of something. When I talk about things like freedom and desert simply as values, I mean to imply that they are standards used by people in general. Judgments using such standards are called *value judgments*.

wellbeing, welfare Whatever is good for someone contributes to their *wellbeing*. Different conceptions of wellbeing arise from different views of what is good for people. Although *welfare* and wellbeing are synonyms, I have tried to follow popular usage by using welfare mainly when talking about the kinds of service provided by the 'welfare state'.

work I include in *work* not just paid employment but also other socially necessary tasks such as the unpaid care of children and old people, and domestic cooking and cleaning.

Do-It-Yourself Equality

I offer the following games and puzzles for the benefit of readers who enjoy working things out for themselves. That, after all, is what equality is all about. Although they all stem from discussions in the text, they are emphatically not 'exercises', and they don't all have answers!

Target Practice

Critically examine the following quotations:

1. 'Are we prepared to urge upon ourselves or our fellows that any person whose wealth exceeds the average of all persons in the world should immediately dispose of the excess by distributing it equally to all the rest of the world's inhabitants?' (Milton Friedman)

2. 'Marx saw merit in feudalism . . . because in a feudal society each man had his own place, and was respected in that place. It is better to be a bathroom attendant in an Oxford college than to be a prosperous proletarian in an amorphous plebs, because the bathroom attendant, although he occupies a relatively lowly position in the college hierarchy, nevertheless is enabled to feel that he is a valued member of that society, making a real and definite contribution to its well-being. In comparison, a modern egalitarian society can be very heartless.' (J.R. Lucas)

3. 'The essential thing is that every citizen should have an equal chance – that is his basic democratic right; but provided the start is fair, let there be maximum scope for advancement.' (C.A.R. Crosland)

4. 'A family is poor if it cannot afford to eat. It is not poor if it cannot afford endless smokes.' (Keith Joseph and Jonathan Sumption)

5. 'See how the Fates their gifts allot,
For A is happy – B is not.
Yet B is worthy, I dare say,
Of more prosperity than A! . . .

B should be happy!
Oh, so happy!
Laughing, Ha! ha!
Chaffing, Ha! ha!
Nectar-quaffing, Ha! ha! ha!
But condemned to die is he,
Wretched, meritorious B!' (W.S. Gilbert)

6. 'Fundamentally, there are only two ways of co-ordinating the economic activities of millions. One is central direction involving the use of coercion – the technique of the army and the modern totalitarian state. The other is the voluntary cooperation of individuals – the technique of the market place.' (Milton Friedman)

7. 'A socialist society would have to forbid capitalist acts between consenting adults.' (Robert Nozick)

8. 'The man who brings home to his wife his weekly earnings, his professional fees, or his share of the profits of a business, merely repeats on a higher scale the action of the lion who carries a deer or an antelope to his den.' (Walter Bagehot, 1870s)

9. 'The building block of nearly all human societies is the nuclear family. The populace of an American industrial city, no less than a band of hunter-gatherers in the Australian desert, is organized around this unit. In both cases . . . the women and children remain in the residential area while the men forage for game or its symbolic equivalent in the form of barter or money.' (E.O. Wilson, 1970s)

Brain Teasers

1. Compulsive gamblers need big bankrolls. Do egalitarians have to oblige?
2. Can a person's wellbeing consist in being better off than everyone else?
3. What is sexist advertising and why is it degrading?
4. Is patriotism itself sickening, or only right-wing patriotism?
5. 'We haven't hired any women because none applied.' Surely *that's* a good excuse?
6. Who deserves more praise: the person who wins a game easily, or the one who loses it after playing very well?
7. Does health and safety legislation restrict economic freedom? Why not?
8. If nationalized industries are so inefficient, why are people so eager to buy them?

Word Games

1. People talk in schools about the needs of 'gifted' children. Are they all real needs?
2. You can exploit both mineral reserves and people. Does that make 'exploit' ambiguous?
3. Is the word 'fraternity' sexist? If so, what word should we use instead?
4. There used to be a popular distinction between the 'deserving poor' and the 'undeserving poor'. What do you think it meant? Is the distinction valid?
5. What is 'free enterprise'? Is it the opposite of unfree enterprise?
6. Is there a difference between selfishness and self-interest? If so, which is more common?

Self-analysis

1. Would you be impressed to meet a Lord? Why?

2. Would you feel uncomfortable using the word 'comrade'? Why?

3. Would you rather get a job through 'open competition' than under a quota system? Why?

4. Do you deserve a higher income?

5. Analyse the freedoms and restraints involved in your present occupation. Would you have more or less freedom in an egalitarian society?

6. How many of the things you own would you be happy to share if you knew you'd still be able to use them? How many of the things owned by other people would you like them to share with you?

7. 'People are learning the price of insurrection and insubordination.' (Ian MacGregor, on the 1984-85 coal strike) How would this kind of manager motivate you?

8. How (if at all) would you consider yourself to be privileged? How many of these privileges depend on other people being unprivileged?

Research Projects

1. Make a list of the people you see sporting superior attitudes, and see how long it takes to find *one* who's right.

2. How many groups can you name which have been called communities? How many of them are?

3. Make a note of every use you hear this week of the concept of desert, and categorize them. What values do the cases of merit desert implicitly appeal to?

4. Try to get something free in a free market.

5. In Mondragon firms the ratio between the pay of the highest-paid managers and the lowest-paid manual workers is about 4.5 to 1. What is it where you work?

6. List ten obvious differences between men and women. How many of them are part of human nature? How do you know?

7. Study your newspaper for a week. How many items encourage people to accept existing inequalities? How many encourage people to reject them?

$64,000 Questions

1. Does anyone really deserve contempt?
2. Can a whole country have a sense of community?
3. How might an egalitarian society deal with the problem of more people wanting to do certain jobs than there was any need for?
4. Could a society function without educational certificates?
5. 'Even if we admit that people can be motivated by a belief in fairness, that doesn't mean that an egalitarian society would succeed. Lots of people think equality is *unfair* – therefore in an egalitarian society they *wouldn't* be motivated to work.' What does this imply about the conditions for having an egalitarian society?
6. In most societies, people are rewarded for accepting the central values and punished for rejecting them. Would an egalitarian society be the same? Would that make it inegalitarian?

References and
Further Reading

This is a selection of works I've found useful. Most of them have their own bibliographies.

General

Practically all recent thinking about equality has been influenced by John Rawls *A Theory of Justice* (Oxford University Press, 1972). Another recent and more egalitarian book is Michael Walzer *Spheres of Justice* (Basic Books, 1983). An earlier but classic defence of equality is R.H. Tawney *Equality* (George Allen & Unwin, 1964). Other useful recent defences of equality include Philip Green *The Pursuit of Inequality* (Martin Robertson, 1981), William Ryan *Equality* (Pantheon, 1981), and Kai Nielson *Equality and Liberty* (Rowman & Allanheld, 1985). Among recent attacks on equality, the cleverest is Robert Nozick *Anarchy, State, and Utopia* (Blackwell, 1974). Others include Keith Joseph and Jonathan Sumption *Equality* (John Murray, 1979), Anthony Flew *The Politics of Procrustes* (Temple Smith, 1981), and William Letwin (ed.) *Against Equality* (Macmillan, 1983), which contains J.R. Lucas 'Against Equality Again', *Philosophy* 52 (1977). Richard Norman *Free and Equal* (Oxford University Press, 1987) is an egalitarian work which appeared while this book was in press.

Chapter 1: What Egalitarians Believe

For theoretical problems in defining equality, see G.W. Mortimore 'An Ideal of Equality', *Mind* 77 (1968), Joseph Raz 'Principles of Equality', *Mind* 87 (1978), Ted Honderich 'The Question of Well-Being and the Principle of Equality', *Mind* 90 (1981), Ronald Dworkin 'What is Equality?' (in two parts), *Philosophy and Public Affairs* 10 (1981), Douglas Rae et al. *Equalities* (Harvard University Press, 1981), Bruce Landesman 'Egalitarianism', *Canadian Journal of Philosophy* 13 (1983), and Michael Walzer *Spheres of Justice* (Basic Books, 1983) chapter 1. The three-way analysis of inequality in terms of wealth, status, and power stems from Max Weber *Economy and Society*, ed. Guenther Roth and Claus Wittich (Bedminster Press, 1968) I.iv.5, II.ix.6, and is emphasized by W.G. Runciman *Relative Deprivation and Social Justice* (Routledge & Kegan Paul, 1966) chapter 3. References on socialism, democracy, and the welfare state are listed under Chapter 8 (p. 175).

Chapter 2: Human Needs

Some useful accounts of the concept of need are David Braybrooke 'Let Needs Diminish that Preferences May Prosper' in American Philosophical Quarterly monograph *Studies in Moral Philosophy* (1968), Richard Wollheim 'Needs, Desires, and Moral Turpitude' in R.S. Peters (ed.) *Nature and Conduct* (Macmillan, 1975), David Miller *Social Justice* (Oxford University Press, 1976) chapter 4, and David Wiggins, 'Claims of Need' in Ted Honderich (ed.) *Morality and Objectivity* (Routledge & Kegan Paul, 1985). There are constructive discussions of many of the problems with need in Raymond Plant, Harry Lesser and Peter Taylor-Gooby *Political Philosophy and Social Welfare* (Routledge & Kegan Paul, 1980) and in Michael Walzer *Spheres of Justice* (Basic Books, 1983) chapter 3. A classic discussion of true and false needs is Herbert Marcuse *One-Dimensional Man* (Routledge & Kegan Paul, 1964) chapter 1. On conceptions of wellbeing, two useful discussions are Henrik von Wright *The Varieties of Goodness* (Routledge & Kegan Paul, 1963) and Thomas Scanlon 'Preference and Urgency', *Journal of Philosophy* 72

(1975). For attacks on need, see Brian Barry *Political Argument* (Routledge & Kegan Paul, 1965) chapter 3 section 5A, chapter 8 section 4, John Rawls *A Theory of Justice* (Oxford University Press, 1972) pp. 315-17, Fred Rosen 'Basic Needs and Justice', *Mind* 86 (1977), and J.R. Lucas 'Against Equality Again', *Philosophy* 52 (1977) section 3. For an impressive attack on equality of welfare, see Ronald Dworkin 'What is Equality?' Part I, *Philosophy and Public Affairs* 10 (1981). The food statistics cited come from *The State of Food and Agriculture 1983* (Food and Agriculture Organization, 1984); for an explanation of hunger, see Susan George and Nigel Paige *Food for Beginners* (Writers and Readers, 1982).

Chapter 3: Mutual Respect

Typical examples of what I've called the philosophical treatment of respect are Bernard Williams 'The Idea of Equality' in P. Laslett and W.G. Runciman (eds) *Philosophy, Politics and Society: Second Series* (Blackwell, 1962), Steven Lukes 'Socialism and Equality' in *Essays in Social Theory* (Macmillan, 1977), and John Rawls *A Theory of Justice* (Oxford University Press, 1972) section 77. These works all draw on Immanuel Kant *Groundwork to a Metaphysic of Morals* (1785), (several editions, for example, H.J. Paton, ed., *The Moral Law*, Hutchinson, 1974). Criticisms are made in John Charvet 'The Idea of Equality as a Substantive Principle', *Political Studies* 17 (1969) and *A Critique of Freedom and Equality* (Cambridge University Press, 1981), and in J.R. Lucas 'Against Equality Again', *Philosophy* 52 (1977). There has been a lot of recent work on the Marxist idea of exploitation. A good review and bibliography is Norman Geras 'The Controversy About Marx and Justice', *New Left Review* 150 (1985). The example quoted is from S. Crine *Dirty Linen* (Low Pay Unit, 1981). On social superiority, see Michael Walzer *Spheres of Justice* (Basic Books, 1983) chapter 11. For a summary of research on the determinants of personal income, see Henry Phelps Brown *The Inequality of Pay* (Oxford University Press, 1977) chapter 9 section 6.

Chapter 4: A Sense of Community

A classic expression of the relation between community and equality is Peter Kropotkin 'Anarchist Morality' in Roger N. Baldwin (ed.) *Kropotkin's Revolutionary Pamphlets* (Dover, 1970); it is also a central theme in R.H. Tawney *Equality* (George Allen & Unwin, 1964) chapter 1. Community is used to criticize John Rawls in Lawrence Crocker 'Equality, Solidarity, and Rawls's Maximin', *Philosophy and Public Affairs* 6 (1977). Community plays an important part in the arguments of Michael Walzer *Spheres of Justice* (Basic Books, 1983) especially chapters 2-3, Raymond Plant et al. *Political Philosophy and Social Welfare* (Routledge & Kegan Paul, 1980) chapters 9-10, and Michael Taylor *Community, Anarchy and Liberty* (Cambridge University Press, 1982). These all give accounts of the concept of community, for which see also Eric Hobsbawm 'The Idea of Fraternity', *New Society* 34 (Nov 1975) and Anne Phillips 'Fraternity' in Ben Pimlott (ed.) *Fabian Essays in Socialist Thought* (Heinemann, 1984). As usual, a criticism is available in J.R. Lucas 'Against Equality Again', *Philosophy* 52 (1977) section 4. Blood donation is the subject of Richard Titmuss *The Gift Relationship* (George Allen & Unwin, 1970).

Chapter 5: Is Equality of Opportunity Enough?

The classic statement of careers open to talents is the *Declaration of the Rights of Man and of Citizens* (1789) article 5. The key American documents on affirmative action are Executive Orders 11246 (1965) and 11375 (1967), and the Department of Labor Revised Order No. 4 (*Code of Federal Regulations*, Title 41, Part 60-2). For British guidelines on positive action, see *Code of Practice: Race Relations* (Commission for Racial Equality, 1983) and Equal Opportunities Commission *Code of Practice* (HMSO, 1985). 'Affirmative' and 'positive' action differ slightly in detail, since the British system seems to allow reverse discrimination in training schemes.

For the problems of defining equal opportunity see John Rawls *A Theory of Justice* (Oxford University Press, 1972) sections 12, 17, 46, Onora O'Neill 'How Do we Know when

Opportunities are Equal?' in Mary Vetterling-Braggin et al. (eds) *Feminism and Philosophy* (Littlefield, Adams, 1977), and Douglas Rae et al. *Equalities* (Harvard University Press) chapter 4. Affirmative action and preferential treatment have been discussed extensively, though not always distinguished. A good defence is Richard A. Wasserstrom 'Preferential Treatment' in *Philosophy and Social Issues* (University of Notre Dame Press, 1980). For a typical attack see Alan H. Goldman 'Affirmative Action', *Philosophy and Public Affairs* 5 (1976). Classic egalitarian attacks on equal opportunity are R.H. Tawney *Equality* (George Allen & Unwin, 1964) chapter 3 section 2, John H. Schaar 'Equality of Opportunity, and Beyond' in J.R. Pennock and J. Chapman (eds) *Equality: Nomos IX* (Atherton, 1967), and Christopher Jencks *Inequality* (Allen Lane, 1974). For an egalitarian criticism of preferential treatment, see Michael Walzer *Spheres of Justice* (Basic Books, 1983) chapter 5.

Chapter 6: Do Some People Deserve More Than Others?

Much recent discussion of desert begins from Joel Feinberg 'Justice and Personal Desert' in *Doing and Deserving* (Princeton University Press, 1970). Subsequent refinements are John Kleinig 'The Concept of Desert', *American Philosophical Quarterly* 8 (1971), David Miller *Social Justice* (Oxford University Press, 1976) chapter 3, James C. Dick 'How to Justify a Distribution of Earnings', *Philosophy and Public Affairs* 2 (1973), and Bruce Landesman 'The Weakness of Desert' (not yet published). A good account of the frontal assault on desert is Brian Barry *Political Argument* (Routledge & Kegan Paul) chapter 6. A good sense of why it doesn't work is provided by P.F. Strawson 'Freedom and Resentment' in *Freedom and Resentment and Other Essays* (Methuen, 1974). The 'services rendered' argument is in Keith Joseph and Jonathan Sumption *Equality* (John Murray, 1979) chapter 4. An interesting view on the role of desert in an egalitarian society is Michael Walzer *Spheres of Justice* (Basic Books, 1983) chapters 5, 6, 11. The figure for average pay comes from *New Earnings Survey* Part A (HMSO, 1984).

Chapter 7: Would Equality Restrict Freedom?

Three modern proponents of the 'freedom versus equality' argument are F.A. Hayek *The Constitution of Liberty* (Routledge & Kegan Paul, 1960) esp. chapter 1 and *Law, Legislation and Liberty, Volume II: The Mirage of Social Justice* (Routledge & Kegan Paul, 1976), Robert Nozick *Anarchy, State and Utopia* (Blackwell, 1974), and Milton Friedman *Capitalism and Freedom* (University of Chicago Press, 1962) esp. chapters 1, 10, 12. What I call the 'standard egalitarian position' is based on R.H. Tawney *Equality* (George Allen & Unwin, 1964) chapters 5 and 7, E.F. Carritt 'Liberty and Equality' in A. Quinton (ed.) *Political Philosophy* (Oxford University Press, 1967), and Richard Norman 'Does Equality Destroy Liberty?' in Keith Graham (ed.) *Contemporary Political Philosophy* (Cambridge University Press, 1982).

For an account of property rights and responsibilities, see A.M. Honoré 'Ownership' in A.G. Guest (ed.) *Oxford Essays in Jurisprudence* (Oxford University Press, 1961); Honoré applies his account to Nozick in 'Property, Title, and Redistribution' in Virginia Held (ed.) *Property, Profits, and Economic Justice* (Wadsworth Publishing Co, 1980). In this chapter, I've drawn on G.A. Cohen's extensive work on the liberty-property-equality issue. See in particular 'Illusions about Private Property and Freedom' in John Mepham and David Hillel-Rubin (eds) *Issues in Marxist Philosophy, Volume IV: Social and Political Philosophy* (Harvester, 1981) and 'Freedom, Justice, and Capitalism', *New Left Review* 126 (1981). On property and power, see Michael Walzer *Spheres of Justice* (Basic Books, 1983) chapter 12.

The quotations concerning political freedom are from J.R. Lucas 'Against Equality Again', *Philosophy* 52 (1977) and Frank Parkin *Class Inequality and Political Order* (Granada, 1972). The statistics on ownership and control of capital are from sources listed under Chapter 9 (p. 177). The statistic for small business failures is based on Department of Trade and Industry research published in Pom Ganguly *UK Small Business Statistics and International Comparisons* (Harper & Row, 1985) chapter 18. The 200-year-old objection can be found in David Hume *An Enquiry Concerning the Principles of Morals* (1751) (various editions, for example, Oxford University Press, 1902) III,ii. The quotation from Marx is from *Capital* Volume I (1867) (various editions, for example, Penguin, 1976) chapter 31. For an argument that a democratic road to socialism is both the correct and the truly Marxist view, see Keith Graham *The Battle of Democracy* (Wheatsheaf, 1986) chapters 9-10.

Chapter 8: Does Society Benefit from Inequality?

For classical utilitarianism, see Jeremy Bentham *An Intro-duction to the Principles of Morals and Legislation* (1789) (various editions, for example, Blackwell, 1948) and John Stuart Mill *Utilitarianism* (1861) (various editions, for example, Fontana, 1962). J.J.C. Smart defends utilitarianism and Bernard Williams attacks it in their book *Utilitarianism: For and Against* (Cambridge University Press, 1973). The 'benefit-all' idea is associated with John Rawls *A Theory of Justice* (Oxford University Press, 1972). But the issue is complicated because Rawls operates with what he calls 'primary social goods' ('rights and liberties, opportunities and powers, income and wealth') rather than in terms of individual wellbeing. Rawls conducts a running battle against utilitarianism, the success of which is queried in K.J. Arrow 'Some Ordinalist-Utilitarian Notes on Rawls's Theory of Justice', *Journal of Philosophy* 70 (1973), David Lyons 'Rawls versus Utilitarian-ism', *Journal of Philosophy* 69 (1972), David Braybrooke 'Utilitarianism with a Difference', *Canadian Journal of Philosophy* 3 (1973), and J.C. Harsanyi 'Can the Maximin Principle Serve as a Basis for Morality?' in *Essays in Ethics, Social Behaviour, and Scientific Explanation* (Reidel, 1976). So much has been written about Rawls that everyone's lost count. Typical egalitarian criticisms are L. Crocker 'Equality, Solidarity, and Rawls's Maximin', *Philosophy and Public Affairs* 6 (1977), C.B. Macpherson 'Rawls's Models of Man and Society', *Philosophy of Social Science* 3 (1973), and Brian Barry *The Liberal Theory of Justice* (Oxford University Press, 1973).

A general attempt to defend equality of a sort (strictly equal incomes) against the charge of inefficiency is Joseph H. Carens *Equality, Moral Incentives, and the Market* (University of Chicago Press, 1981). There are useful discussions of motivation in Amartya K. Sen 'Rational Fools: A Critique of the Behavioural Foundations of Economic Theory', *Philosophy and Public Affairs* 6 (1977), John Kenneth Galbraith *The New Industrial State* (Hamilton, 1967) chapters 11-13, and Robert Goodin *Political Theory and Public Policy* (University of Chicago Press, 1982) chapter 6. Statistics on overtime and bonus payments are from *New Earnings Survey* Part A (HMSO, 1984); on managerial pay, from the Royal Commission on the Distribution of Income and Wealth *Report No. 3. Higher Incomes from Employment* (Cmnd. 6383, HMSO, 1976). For information on incentive schemes, see R.H.S. Beecham *Pay Schemes: Principles and Techniques* (Heinemann, 1979). Part of my discussion of incentives is expanded in 'Incentives for Equality' (not yet published). The study on child care quoted is David Piachaud *Round About Fifty Hours a Week* (Child Poverty Action Group, 1984). Typical discussions of motivation from a management perspective are Gerald Silver *Introduction to Management* (West Publishing Co, 1981) chapter 15 and Richard M. Steers and Lyman W. Porter *Motivation and Work Behaviour* (3rd edition, McGraw Hill, 1983). On the necessity of hierarchy in the capitalist firm, see Stephen A. Marglin 'What Do Bosses Do?', *Journal of Radical Political Economics* 6 (1974), reprinted in André Gorz (ed.) *The Division of Labour* (Harvester, 1976); and Samuel Bowles 'The Production Process in a Competitive Economy', *American Economic Review* 75 (1985). On co-operatives, see Jenny Thornley *Workers' Cooperatives: Jobs and Dreams* (Heinemann Educational Books, 1982) and Robert Jackall & Henry M. Levin (eds) *Worker Cooperatives in America* (University of California Press, 1984). The study of Mondragon cited is Keith Bradley and Alan Gelb *Cooperation at Work: The Mondragon Experience* (Heinemann Educational Books, 1983). See also Henk Thomas and Chris Logan *Mondragon: An Economic Analysis* (George Allen & Unwin, 1982). On China and Cuba, see Charles Hoffmann *The Chinese Worker* (State University of New York Press, 1974), C. Riskin 'Maoism and Motivation' in V. Nee and J. Peck (eds) *China's Uninterrupted Revolution* (Pantheon, 1975), Roberto M. Bernardo *Popular Management and Pay in China* (University of the Philippines Press, 1977) and *The Theory of Moral Incentives in Cuba* (University of Alabama Press, 1971), and Carmelo Mesa-Lago *The Labor Sector and Socialist Distribution in Cuba* (Praeger, 1968). For an egalitarian comparison and criticism of both capitalist and non-capitalist systems see Samuel Farber 'Material and Non-Material Work Incentives as

Ideologies and Practices of Order', *Review of Radical Political Economics* 14 (1982).

An example of an egalitarian and participatory approach to welfare services is Peter Beresford and Suzy Croft *Whose Welfare?* (Lewis Cohen Urban Studies Centre, 1986). The classical argument that capitalism requires poverty and unemployment is Marx *Capital* Volume I (1867) (various editions, e.g. Penguin, 1976) chapters 23-25. On capitalism and needs, see Herbert Marcuse *One-Dimensional Man* (Routledge & Kegan Paul, 1964) and Raymond Plant et al. *Political Philosophy and Social Welfare* (Routledge & Kegan Paul, 1980). A recent defence of democratic planning for real needs is Stephen Bodington, Mike George and John Michaelson *Developing the Socially Useful Economy* (Macmillan, 1986). General philosophical discussions of the role of markets can be found in Rawls *A Theory of Justice* sections 41-43, Michael Walzer *Spheres of Justice* (Basic Books, 1983) chapter 4, and Plant et al. *Political Philosophy and Social Welfare* chapter 8. For the debate on market socialism, see Oskar Lange 'On the Economic Theory of Socialism' (1936-37) reprinted in Oskar Lange and Fred M. Taylor *On the Economic Theory of Socialism* (McGraw Hill, 1964), Alec Nove *The Economics of Feasible Socialism* (George Allen & Unwin, 1983), Boris Frankel *Beyond the State?* (Macmillan, 1983) chapter 12, Geoff Hodgson *The Democratic Economy* (Penguin, 1984), and Ernest Mandel 'In Defence of Socialist Planning', *New Left Review* 159 (1986). Frankel and Nove exchange views in *Radical Philosophy* 39 (1985). Nove replies to Mandel in *New Left Review* 161 (1987).

On democratic participation, see the following: Carole Pateman *Participation and Democratic Theory* (Cambridge University Press, 1970), Dennis F. Thompson *The Democratic Citizen* (Cambridge University Press, 1970), Benjamin R. Barber *Strong Democracy* (University of California Press, 1984), particularly chapter 10, Walzer *Spheres of Justice* chapter 12, and Keith Graham *The Battle of Democracy* (Wheatsheaf, 1986).

Chapter 9: Is Equality Possible?

The discussion of the !Kung is based primarily on Richard B. Lee *The !Kung San: Men, Women and Work in a Foraging*

Society (Cambridge University Press, 1979), from which the quotations are taken (pp.244-245). See also Lorna Marshall *The !Kung of Nyae Nyae* (Harvard University Press, 1976), Richard B. Lee and Irven DeVore (eds) *Kalahari Hunter-Gatherers* (Harvard University Press, 1976), Patricia Draper '!Kung Women' in Rayna R. Reiter (ed.) *Toward an Anthropology of Women* (Monthly Review Press, 1975), Marjorie Shostak *Nisa: The Life and Words of a !Kung Woman* (Harvard University Press, 1981), and Ron E. Roberts and Douglas E. Brintnall *Reinventing Inequality* (Schenkman, 1982). For other anthropological material, see Judith K. Brown 'Iroquois Women' also in Reiter, Eleanor Burke Leacock *Myths of Male Dominance* (Monthly Review Press, 1981), Elizabeth Friedl *Women and Men: An Anthropologist's View* (Holt, Rinehart and Winston, 1975), Frances Dahlberg (ed.) *Woman the Gatherer* (Yale University Press, 1981), and Marshall Sahlins 'The Sociology of Primitive Exchange' in *Stone Age Economics* (Aldine-Atherton, 1972). Henry Phelps Brown *The Inequality of Pay* (Oxford University Press, 1977) chapter 4 section 6 draws on Richard B. Lee and Irven DeVore (eds) *Man the Hunter* (Aldine, 1968) and M.G. Bicchieri (ed.) *Hunters and Gatherers Today* (Holt, Rinehart, & Winston, 1972). Historical and anthropological material features strongly in Michael Walzer *Spheres of Justice* (Basic Books, 1983) and Michael Taylor *Community, Anarchy and Liberty* (Cambridge University Press, 1982). For psychological evidence, see Eleanor Emmons Maccoby and Carol Nagy Jacklin *The Psychology of Sex Differences* (Stanford University Press, 1974). Melvin Konner's *The Tangled Wing* (Penguin, 1984) is a readable but not always convincing attempt to synthesize relevant anthropology, psychology, and biology.

Of the many criticisms of male dominance, some good starting points are Naomi Wiesstein '"Kinde, Kuche, Kirche" as Scientific Law: Psychology Constructs the Female' in Robin Morgan (ed.) *Sisterhood is Powerful* (Vintage, 1970), Ann Oakley *Sex, Gender and Society* (Temple Smith, 1972), Caroline Whitbeck 'Theories of Sex Difference' and Carol Gould 'The Woman Question', both in C.C. Gould and M. Wartofsky (eds) *Women and Philosophy* (Pantheon, 1976), Joyce Trebilcot 'Sex Roles: The Argument from Nature' and Christine Pierce 'Natural Law Language and Women', both in Jane English (ed.) *Sex Equality* (Prentice-Hall, 1977), Anne Dickason 'The Feminine as Universal' in Mary Vetterling-

Braggin et al. (eds) *Feminism and Philosophy* (Littlefield, Adams, 1977), Janet Sayers *Biological Politics* (Tavistock, 1982), and Philip Green *The Pursuit of Inequality* (Martin Robertson, 1981) chapter 5, who also discusses similar theories of racial differences, open to the same kinds of general argument, in chapter 3. On these, see also Richard A. Wasserstrom 'Racism and Sexism' in *Philosophy and Social Issues* (University of Notre Dame Press, 1980) and William Ryan *Equality* (Pantheon, 1981).

The functionalism/conflict distinction can be found in various textbooks, e.g. Beth E. Vanfossen *The Structure of Social Inequality* (Little, Brown, 1979) and Andrew Blowers et al. *Patterns of Inequality Units 1-2: The Importance of Social Inequality* (Open University Press, 1976). The functionalist theory of inequality is classically expressed in Kingsley Davis and Wilbert E. Moore 'Some Principles of Stratification' in R. Bendix and S.M. Lipset (eds) *Class, Status and Power* (2nd edition, Routledge & Kegan Paul, 1967). For a selection of readings, see M.M. Tumin (ed.) *Readings on Social Stratification* (Prentice-Hall, 1970), in which G. Huaco 'The Functionalist Theory of Stratification: Two Decades of Controversy' reviews the literature. Marxism is of course a prime example of a 'conflict' theory, exemplified in Karl Marx and Friedrich Engels *The Communist Manifesto* (1848) (various editions, e.g. Penguin, 1973). An important non-Marxist conflict theorist is Ralf Dahrendorf *Class and Class Conflict in Industrial Society* (Routledge & Kegan Paul, 1959) and 'On the Origin of Social Inequality' in P. Laslett and W. Runciman *Philosophy, Politics and Society: second series* (Blackwell, 1962).

Sources for the statistics are, for the UK: Royal Commission on the Distribution of Income and Wealth *An A to Z of Income and Wealth* (HMSO, 1980) and *Report No. 7: Fourth Report on the Standing Reference* (Cmnd. 7595, HMSO, 1979) chapter 6; John Scott *The Upper Classes* (Macmillan, 1982) chapters 6-7; and L.R. Klein et al. 'Savings and Finances of the Upper Income Classes', *Bulletin of the Oxford University Institute of Statistics* November 1956. *Business Monitor: Company Finance* (16th issue: HMSO, 1985) shows that in 1981 the 2,213 'large' non-financial companies (companies with over £4.16m capital employed) accounted for nearly 90 per cent of all company assets. Statistics for the US come from Thomas R. Dye *Who's Running America?* (2nd edition,

Prentice-Hall, 1979), Louis Kriesberg *Social Equality* (Prentice-Hall, 1979) chapter 3, Wilbur G. Lewellen *The Ownership Income of Management* (National Bureau of Economic Research, 1971) chapter 1, and *Statistical Abstract of the United States: 1985* (US Bureau of the Census, 1985). Figures for offical development aid come from Rutherford M. Poats *Twenty-five Years of Development Co-operation: A Review* (OECD, 1985).

On the relationship between capitalism, skilled work, and technology see Mike Cooley *Architect or Bee?* (Hand and Brain, 1980). For an analysis of the power of anti-egalitarians in the UK see Ralph Miliband *The State in Capitalist Society* (Weidenfeld & Nicolson, 1969) or *Marxism and Politics* (Oxford University Press, 1977), Scott *The Upper Classes* chapters 6-7, John Westergaard and Henrietta Resler *Class in a Capitalist Society* (Penguin, 1975), and David Coates, Gordon Johnston and Ray Bush (eds) *A Socialist Anatomy of Britain* (Polity Press, 1985), which also gives a valuable picture of the condition of the British Left. The classic analysis of the problem of collective action is Mancur Olson *The Logic of Collective Action* (Harvard University Press, 1965). For applications to socialist politics see Alan Buchanan 'Revolutionary Motivation and Rationality', *Philosophy and Public Affairs* 9 (1979) and Jon Elster *Making Sense of Marx* (Cambridge University Press & Editions de la Maison des Sciences de l'Homme, 1985) section 6.2.

Chapter 10: Miscellaneous Objections

On equality and culture, see R.H. Tawney *Equality* (George Allen & Unwin, 1964) chapter 2 section iii. For statistical sources, see references for Chapter 9 (page 177). The argument on why equality matters follows John Westergaard and Henrietta Resler *Class in a Capitalist Society* (Penguin, 1975); an unexpected example of the view that it doesn't matter is Alec Nove *Feasible Socialism* (George Allen & Unwin, 1983) Part 4. On envy, see John Rawls *A Theory of Justice* (Oxford University Press, 1972) sections 80-81, who cites Helmut Schoeck *Envy: A Theory of Social Behaviour* trans. Michael Glenny and Betty Ross (Secker & Warburg, 1969) chapters 14-15 for the anti-egalitarian view. There's also a discussion in Robert Nozick *Anarchy, State, and Utopia* (Blackwell, 1974) chapter 8.

On philosophical method, a more developed account of my own view is given in John Baker 'Mill's Captivating "Proof" and the Foundations of Ethics', *Social Theory and Practice* 6 (1980). The general position is not very different from many other philosophers, of whom one of the best examples is Bernard Williams *Ethics and the Limits of Philosophy* (Fontana, 1985). Other useful starting points might be Brian Barry *Political Argument* (Routledge & Kegan Paul, 1965) pp. 1-8, 286-91, J.O. Urmson 'A Defence of Intuitionism', *Proceedings of the Aristotelian Society* 75 (1974-75), or even Michael Oakeshott 'Political Education' in *Rationalism in Politics* (Methuen, 1962).

Glossary

Authors cited are Marx *Capital* volume I (1867) (various editions, for example, Penguin, 1976), Max Weber *Economy and Society*, ed. Gunther Roch and Claus Wittich (Bedminster Press, 1968) I.iv.5, II.ix.6, Casey Miller and Kate Swift *The Handbook of Non-Sexist Writing* (Women's Press, 1981), and Steven Lukes *Individualism* (Blackwell, 1973). The term 'meritocracy' was invented by Michael Young in *The Rise of the Meritocracy* (Penguin, 1970).

Do-It-Yourself Equality

The authors cited are Friedman *Capitalism and Freedom* (University of Chicago Press, 1962); Lucas 'Against Equality Again', *Philosophy* 52 (1977); Anthony Crosland *The Future of Socialism* (Jonathan Cape, 1956) as quoted in Steven Lukes 'Socialism and Equality' in *Essays in Social Theory* (Macmillan, 1977); Keith Joseph and Jonathan Sumption *Equality* (John Murray, 1979); W.S. Gilbert *The Savoy Operas* (Macmillan, 1959); Robert Nozick *Anarchy, State and Utopia* (Blackwell, 1974); Walter Bagehot 'Biology and Women's Rights', *Popular Science Monthly* 14 (1879) and E.O. Wilson *Sociobiology: The New Synthesis* (Harvard University Press, 1975), both quoted in Janet Sayers *Biological Politics* (Tavistock, 1982); Ian MacGregor as quoted in Geoffrey Goodman *The Miners' Strike* (Pluto, 1985).

Index

NOTE: items marked * appear in the glossary